2

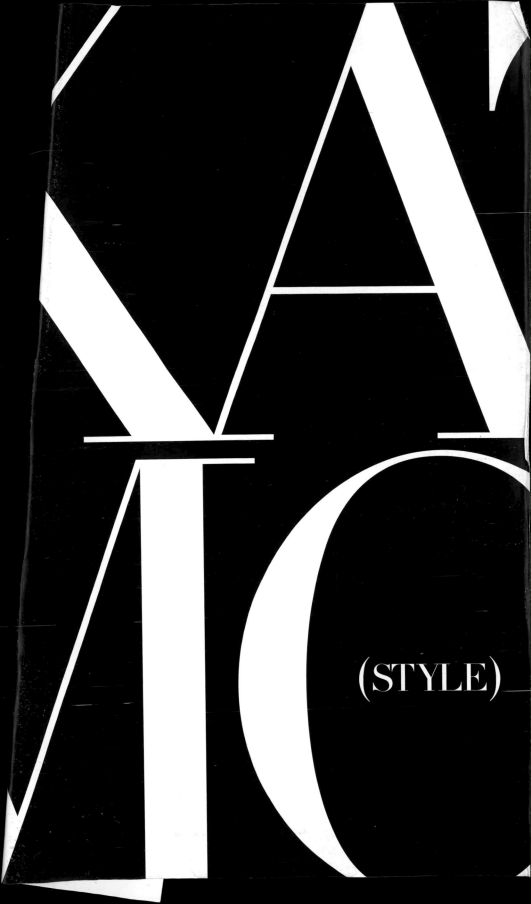

(STYLE)

Published by Century 2008

2 4 6 8 10 9 7 5 3 1

First published in Great Britain in 2008 by
Century
Random House, 20 Vauxhall Bridge Road,
London SW1V 2SA

www.rbooks.co.uk

Addresses for companies within The Random House Group Limited can be found at:
www.randomhouse.co.uk

The Random House Group Limited Reg. No. 954009

A CIP catalogue record for this book
is available from the British Library

ISBN HB 9781846054297
ISBN TPB 9781846054303

The Random House Group Limited supports The Forest Stewardship
Council (FSC), the leading international forest certification organisation. All our
titles that are printed on Greenpeace approved FSC certified paper carry the FSC logo. Our
paper procurement policy can be found at www.rbooks.co.uk/environment

Printed and bound in Germany by
Appl, Aprinta Druck, Wemding

# KATE MOSS STYLE

C

CENTURY

This book is dedicated to:
my 'prayer square': Esther Adams, Debs Gardner-Paterson,
Jennifer Jamie and Lucinda Lloyd – the coolest girls in the whole world.
Thanks for keeping me sane. x


And, of course, to Kate Moss
for making fashion
so much fun for everyone.

**My grateful thanks to the following:**

Charlotte Haycock, my editor at Random House,
for giving me the opportunity to write my dream book.

My literary agent Gordon Wise at Curtis Brown
for staying cool, calm and collected.

Alex Butt for making ten million phone calls and making
this happen (and making me laugh).

Andrew and Jenny Diprose for achieving the impossible and designing
a book that looks as sexy and elegant as Ms Moss herself.

Anna Dewhurst for putting her Olsen twins obsession on hold for long
enough to find all the brilliant images in this book.

Liza Bruce and Tracey Tolkien, for their fascinating insights into
Kate's take on fashion, which have been crucial in shaping this book.

Steve Cole, Chidi Achara, Amanda King, Morgan Holden-White, Andy McConkey, Anne Ayles,
Allison Troup-Jensen, and all my friends at Artisan Initiatives and St Mary's Bryanston Square, who
prayed for me throughout this entire journey.

Esther and Jonny Grant, for always being there for me, even from
the other side of the world. I miss you every day.

My family: Mum and Dad, Jon, Lorna, and Ruby for always giving
me encouragement and support, and (even better!) space.

**I would also like to thank:**

Jennifer Broadley for being the best business coach a writer could wish for.
Andrew Tucker, my wonderfully wise friend and mentor.
Rebecca-Lucy Innes, for preliminary research.
Grazia girls Jane Bruton, Lucy Dunn, and Melanie Rickey for all their support
(and pretending to miss me), and particularly Catherine Nieto for
knowing everyone in Fashionland.
My TV agents, Jacquie Drewe and Jessica Hanscom at Curtis Brown,
for letting me hit the pause button.
The unstoppable Gok Wan for waiting for me.
Jo Whiley, for putting up with months of my Kate-induced dementia
(and still being hotter than Moss).
My French 'prof' Simon Brewer, and James and Janie Cronin for
translations; merci beaucoup.
The astonishing Kitty Tebbetts for her party-planning prowess.
Steph and Jonna Sercombe for meals on wheels (especially the 'love-sagna').
Bernie Gardner  and Davey Spens for entertaining interruptions.
Ben Jamie for shooting me.
Tim Lusher and Richartd Hughes for a little help from my friends.

# ABOUT THE AUTHOR

Angela Buttolph lives and works in London. A graduate of the London College of Fashion, she has written for every major fashion magazine, from Vogue to i-D, and is the co-author of Phaidon's Fashion Book. She is now a contributing editor for Grazia. An experienced broadcaster, she has also presented a number of fashion shows, from ITV1's Hollywood Star Treatment to BBC2's A Week of Dressing Dangerously, and is currently Radio 1's Fashion Expert, giving style advice to the 4 million listeners of Jo Whiley's Morning Show.

www.AngelaButtolph.com

# INTRODUCTION

Earlier this year Kate Moss was asked in an interview if she was born cool. Kate just laughed.

This book attempts to answer that question.

What makes a style icon?

I don't mean which approach to dressing. But which events, relationships and other influences have to collide in order to turn someone into not just a stylish dresser, but a style icon?

Over the years, countless people have declared that Kate just has 'innate good taste' or 'a natural sense of style'.

But still, I wanted to know. And because I wanted to know, I wrote this book. I've traced Kate's style through the years, across continents, in and out of trends.

I wanted to get inside not just Kate's wardrobe, but inside her head.

Kate's adventures in dressing tell us something about fashion, and quite a lot about her. She has had the kind of fashion education the rest of us can only dream of; a unique experience in the industry which is unlikely to happen ever again.

She is beautiful, a size 6, a multi-millionairess. And yet, I believe that there is still something we can learn from her experiences.

For years we've wanted to dress how Kate dresses. But perhaps the real trick is to learn how to think how Kate thinks about clothes.

Because if there's one thing Kate would never been caught dead doing, it's copying someone else's style.

CONTENTS

Introduction 1
In Suburbia 4
About a girl 14
The London Look 28
LA Story 56
Kate Britannia 82
Changes 94
Style Icon 118
With the Band 136
Shop Girl 166
Fashionably 182
Ever After
Epilogue 198
Contributors 200

# 1
# In Suburbia

'I was just like my friends in Croydon,
James Brown and the posse.
They were really fashion-conscious
because they were suburban,
and that's the way suburban people
are. They're more fashion-
conscious, and they're more trendy.'
KATE MOSS

any extraordinary stories have ordinary beginnings. And life doesn't get more ordinary than British suburbia. Croydon, in South London, is a bleak concrete tangle of tower blocks, grey office complexes, ugly shopping centres and endless roundabouts. Not exactly the natural environment in which to nurture a world-class style icon. But it was here that Katherine Ann Moss was born on 16 January 1974.

Of course, everything about Kate Moss defies logic: the global trendsetter who stays at the cutting edge of fashion by wearing vintage clothes from decades ago; the style icon as revered for her scruffy 'undone glamour' as she is for her red carpet sophistication; the short, flat-chested, gawky schoolgirl with bandy legs and jagged teeth, who became more sought after than the ultra-beautiful curvaceous supermodels.

Yet, according to Kate, Croydon was the perfect place to become style-savvy: 'That's the way suburban people are; they're more fashion-conscious, and they're more trendy.' For the affluent middle-class teenagers growing up in boom-time 1980s Britain, the ultimate look to aspire to was flashy designer labels, and in Croydon one label in particular.

At eleven, Kate experienced a seminal style moment that left a lasting impression. 'I remember seeing that model Keith Martin on the bus on the way home from school head to toe in Westwood, you know, with, like, the Buffalo hat on and the crown. On the bus!'

Kate would develop a lifelong appreciation for the flamboyant, post-punk clothes of British designer Vivienne Westwood. In fact, Kate had already experimented with her own version of Westwood's signature look: 'I remember dressing as a punk aged ten; green lipstick, backcombed hair, Mum's T-shirt as a dress.'

By the late 1980s, while still at secondary school, she was wearing the label herself. 'I was fourteen; in Croydon it was all about Vivienne Westwood. It was like, a crotch [length] mini and a Vivienne Westwood T-shirt, and you know, the proper Sex shoes. That was the look, it was really trendy.'

Label-obsessed, but with a teenager's clothing allowance, Kate was too skint to buy more than the odd designer piece, and was forced to resort to more modest shopping. 'I was always the one in Croydon walking down the street with bags full of Oxfam clothes for 10p. I could always find more than anyone else.'

Kate's style ideas had been inspired by the older kids at school, one of whom would play a key part in her life, from influencing her look to working alongside her in her career, as well as growing to be her best friend and constant companion throughout her life.

James Brown's younger sister Marina was in Kate's class at Riddlesdown High School. Their family lived near to Kate's, not in a grim tower block, but on the same quiet, leafy street of pretty, semi-detached houses. 'A comfortable middle-class background,' according to Kate.

Even at school, James recalls the younger girl stood out. 'Kate hung out with the coolest kids. There were four years between us, but when we had something, two months later, her gang had the same thing. Whether it was the Vivienne Westwood shoes, or asymmetric haircuts…'

Brown's influence on Kate endured; and in

A school photo
in the 1970s.

2001, she proudly told American *Vogue* that, growing up, 'I was just like my friends in Croydon, James Brown and the posse. They were really fashion-conscious.'

Before long, Kate was hanging out with the older kids outside school. When she was in her early teens, her parents, Linda and Peter, split. Kate went to live with her mother, and her younger brother Nick moved in with their father.

After that, everything changed. 'Literally, my parents let me do whatever I wanted. I was smoking when I was thirteen in front of my parents, and drinking,' says Kate. 'I'd have parties where I'd come in at three in the morning. It's actually worked out to my benefit because you end up thinking for yourself because you know you're not rebelling against anything.'

Brown recalls meeting Kate one night, in a cool bar in Croydon. 'It was really a shock to see her there ... she was fourteen!' But Kate looked the part, in jeans and a white vest, with 'bright red lips and fabulous long hair. She had those black Katharine Hamnett boots with the thick heels, and a Goose jacket in leather from New York that I'd been wanting for a year. It was the thing everyone wanted.'

Better travelled than her peers thanks to her dad's job as a travel executive, yearly trips to Disneyland and beyond provided Kate with shopping and people-watching opportunities out of the reach of many of her friends. In the States, she noted, unimpressed, 'everyone wore stone-washed jeans and trainers'.

But it was in America that something happened to Kate that would change her life, and the course of fashion history, forever.

In the summer of 1988, Kate was sitting on a

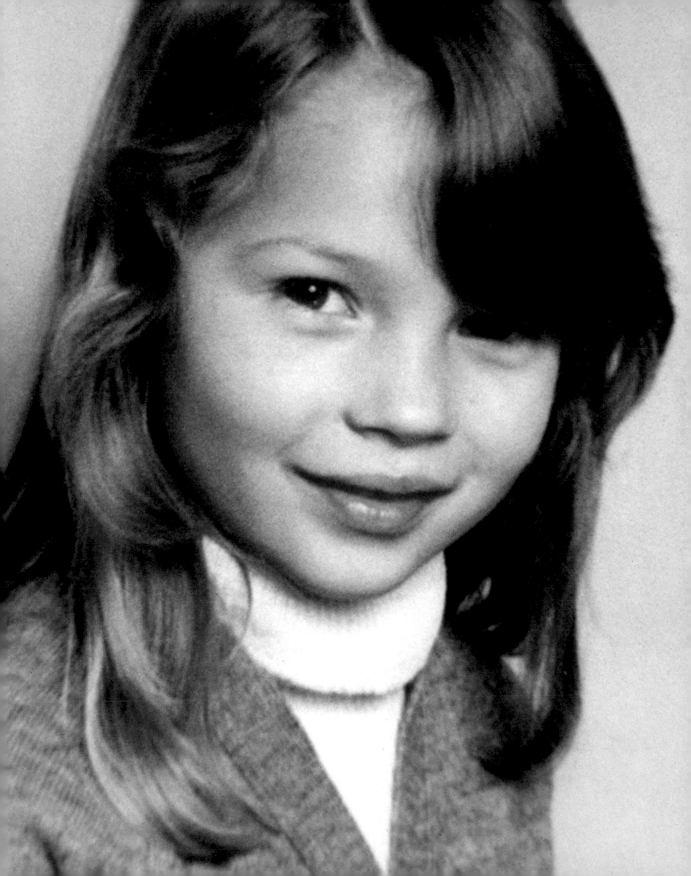

suitcase, plugged into her Walkman, waiting in the Virgin Atlantic standby ticket queue at New York's JFK Airport. After returning from a trip to the Bahamas with her father and brother, the group had found themselves stranded at the airport overnight.

It was at that moment that London model scout Sarah Doukas spotted Kate in a sea of faces, and was instantly struck: 'She had a kind of ethereal look about her, a translucency and such phenomenal bone structure.' Kate was simply but stylishly dressed, wearing 'a white shirt and jeans; I felt very cool.' Even at a young age, James recalls that Kate 'had her own sense of style and was one step ahead of everyone else. I don't know where it came from.'

Anyone who has ever met Kate's mother Linda might have a theory about that. The bone structure, the pretty pout and elfin nose are carbon copies of Linda's, as is the subtle colouring; the mousey 'cup of tea' hair and the hazel eyes. 'Kate's mother is equally stunning,' confirms fashion designer Tom Ford.

Linda's quiet elegance hints at a keen interest in fashion. Before getting married, Linda ran a boutique and worked as an assistant to a knitwear designer. 'It's about taste,' Kate would say later of her own sense of style. 'You've either got good taste or bad taste, and it doesn't matter where you come from,' which may be true geographically, if not genetically. 'I like clothes,' admits Linda. 'I'd like to think that Kate got her sense of style from me. Yes, I would hope so.'

When Kate told her mother of the encounter with Sarah Doukas, Linda was unconvinced that her daughter was model material. But perhaps the signs were there all along. With hindsight, Kate said, 'I've got pictures of me when I was around eleven, posing. Not with the pseudo-model pose, you know, the arm behind the head and all that, but like a real model pose. I don't know why.' They made an appointment and appeared at the agency a week later. Kate was signed on the spot.

'They took some Polaroids, put them in a book, and immediately sent me off on castings. At the end of that first day my mum said, 'If you want to do this, you're on your own because I'm not traipsing around London ever again like that. It's a nightmare.' But within her first week of castings, Kate was booked for a beauty shoot for teenage magazine *Mizz,* posing with a facial scrub for 'like a hundred quid'.

Sarah Doukas's new model agency, Storm, was still getting established, and she had commissioned aspiring fashion photographer David Ross to take test photographs of new models.

The photographer recalls opening his door one day to see what he assumed was a lost child looking for her mother in the wrong flat. 'But it was Kate,' he says. 'It was the autumn half-term holidays and she'd come up to London from Croydon by herself on the train for the photoshoot.' Horrified, David turned her away, asking her to come back with a chaperone. Kate returned the next day with a friend from school.

Back then, Ross was unimpressed by Kate's style credentials: 'She was wearing her own clothes [for the shoot]. It was 1988, but her clothes were from 1986; clothes that were at least a year out of date.'

Kate's latest charity shop purchases included a shoulder-padded double-breasted jacket, a ribbed polo neck sweater and an oversized black parachute silk shirt. The only sign of Kate's love of labels was a sweatshirt emblazoned with a giant Fred Perry logo, and Ross recalls, 'She was wearing baggy trousers that narrowed around the ankles, flat pumps and a dodgy hat.' A look, he says, that 'would only have been good for *Just Seventeen* magazine'.

According to Ross, 'What was really happening then, was short, very high-waisted stretchy skirts, court shoes – I wanted legs.' Although Ross admits, 'It would have been wrong to make her sexy. Pouty was about as sexy as you were going to get.'

But Kate wasn't into the body-conscious styles of the day: 'I was always in jumble sales and Oxfam and not getting things that were on the rack, because I didn't like what was on the rack at the time – kind of 1980s stuff.'

Ross shot the photographs on the roof of his building, heavily directing the aspiring model. 'Without direction, she would just sit there blankly, not knowing what to do. She didn't seem like one of these girls who practised posing in the mirror.' Equally problematic was Kate's height, two inches shorter than the 5' 8" minimum required for models, 'but I thought maybe she'd grow'.

Kate had recognised Sarah Doukas on their first encounter from an interview on *The Clothes Show,* but she admits, 'I didn't know that much about [the fashion world]. I suppose I had ideas about it, but I didn't think about it at all. I'd watched model competitions and *Miss World* on television and things like that, but I wasn't conscious of fashion magazines. I knew teenage magazines.'

By then, James had left school and had started working at a hair salon in Croydon. Hanging out

One of the very first test shots taken by David Ross.

Opposite: On a family holiday.

in the same venues, at the same parties, the pair quickly became close friends. 'If we went out, I'd do her hair, and all her mates' hair. It was always very simple,' says Brown.

When he moved to the Zoo salon in London's Covent Garden, Kate would travel into London with him, often changing out of her school uniform on the train. 'I was testing and stuff when I was fourteen,' said Kate years later, 'and then I did teenage magazines.' From then on, Kate got into the habit of hanging around the salon nearly every day, sitting on the washing machine at the back of the shop. 'Having just started I didn't have very many clients and she didn't have many castings,' said James, 'and as neither of us had any money we were happy hanging around drinking coffee all day long.'

Occasionally he would even accompany Kate on castings, and remembers an early encounter with a photographer who looked at her, saying, 'You're nothing but a common slut; you'll never be successful.' Far from being offended, according to James, she found it hilarious: 'She was doubled up with laughter.'

Kate admits, 'When I started modelling, I really didn't care if I got rejected … I was just having a laugh.' But she was about to meet someone who would change all that.

# 2

## About a
## girl

'I upgraded from jumble sales
to Portobello Market ... and
that's when you start throwing
things together like that'
KATE MOSS

Shopping for clothes at a market in Paris, 1993.

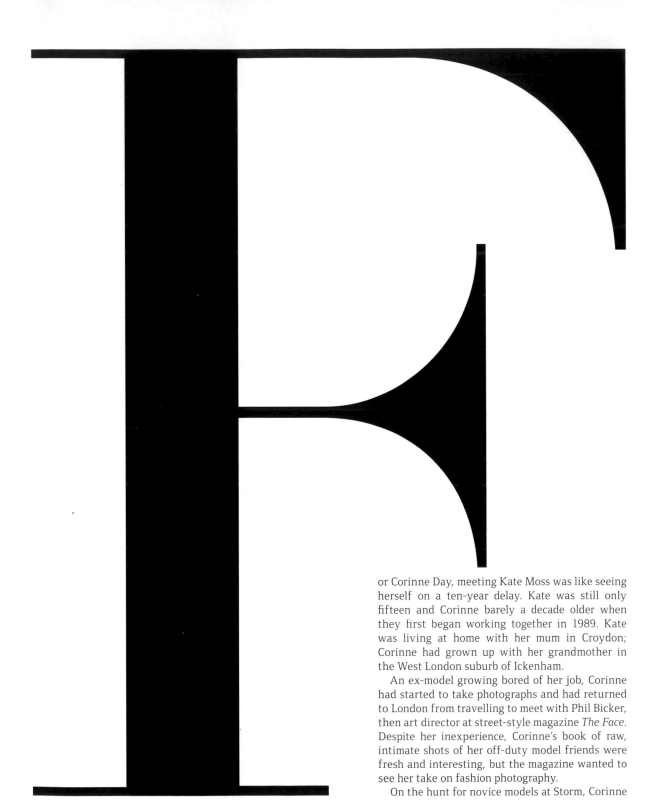

or Corinne Day, meeting Kate Moss was like seeing herself on a ten-year delay. Kate was still only fifteen and Corinne barely a decade older when they first began working together in 1989. Kate was living at home with her mum in Croydon; Corinne had grown up with her grandmother in the West London suburb of Ickenham.

An ex-model growing bored of her job, Corinne had started to take photographs and had returned to London from travelling to meet with Phil Bicker, then art director at street-style magazine *The Face*. Despite her inexperience, Corinne's book of raw, intimate shots of her off-duty model friends were fresh and interesting, but the magazine wanted to see her take on fashion photography.

On the hunt for novice models at Storm, Corinne

On the catwalk at the
John Galliano spring/
summer show, 1990.

Shopping for
clothes at a market
in Paris, 1993.

'SHE EVEN BUYS CLOTHES AND ACCESSORIES IN FLEA MARKETS AND SHE WEARS THEM IN SUCH A FABULOUS AND PERSONAL WAY THAT MAKES MOST OF HER LOOKS IRRESISTIBLE.'

Stefano Gabbana, fashion designer, Dolce & Gabbana, Milan

stumbled across an out-of-focus picture of Kate, and was intrigued enough to request a casting.

There was an instant connection. 'I felt comfortable with her; I could see a bit of myself in her: she's skinny and short and I'm skinny and short,' Day remembers. 'I liked the way she was natural; she hadn't modelled at all, so she was quite carefree. She wasn't conscious of the way she looked or anything like that.'

By the time Corinne was on the scene, Kate had been signed to Storm for only a few months, but was already familiar with the daily grind that makes up the life of a model. 'I went on eight go-sees a day … and it was hideous. No one wanted to know.' Broke, she was working part time in a newsagent.

But the streetwise attitude she was developing was appealing to Day. 'I found her quite cheeky and cocky, and she had a real personality, which is unusual for a girl so young.'

Kate's charity shop wardrobe also struck a chord; Corinne had a lifelong mania for collecting second-hand clothes.

Needing to shoot fashion for *The Face* but not having many contacts within the industry to borrow samples, Corinne improvised. 'Because we were new, it was hard for us to get designer clothes. So we'd go to markets and second-hand shops and we'd just make up fashion that we liked.'

Their first shoot took place in the suburban front garden of Corinne's childhood home, and the clothes were equally unpretentious: 'simple, V-neck jumpers, Kickers from The Natural Shoe Store, and a bias-cut, John Galliano maxi skirt [borrowed] from Browns.'

But Corinne wasn't focusing on the clothes and, unlike Ross, 'I didn't direct her. I wanted to just photograph her as herself, to try and get it as documentary as possible. And get her character and her presence in the pictures. Because fashion [photography] really wasn't about that in the 1980s; it was all about the photographer. I wanted to reverse that and make it about the model.'

Phil Bicker saw something compelling in Day's intimate approach, and would later publish a single shot from the shoot in *The Face*'s March 1990 issue, Kate's debut in the magazine. Within a couple of months, Corinne was commissioned to photograph eight pages of fashion for *The Face*.

Days later, Corinne was walking down Soho's Old Compton Street with a friend, who was telling her about a stylist she knew called Melanie Ward, who, like Corinne and Kate, collected second-hand clothes. Returning down the street later the same day, they bumped into Melanie. 'We went for a coffee and talked about our common interests in second-hand clothes,' says Corinne. 'I asked Melanie if she would like to work with Kate and me for *The Face*.'

Corinne moved to London, and she and Melanie became close friends. They scoured Portobello and Camden Markets every weekend, and trawled charity stores, and second-hand clothing shops like Glorious Clothing in Islington and Cornucopia in Pimlico. 'We worked very closely together,' says Corinne. 'Both of us being on the dole, we shared the expense of buying clothes. I always bought clothes that I would wear myself.'

So it was Corinne choosing Kate's clothes for her, and sharing her wardrobe with Kate; although the idea was to make the clothes in the shoots look like Kate's own, they were Corinne's and Melanie's. Corinne and Melanie were dressing Kate in their style.

'I was only fifteen then, I didn't have any style,' admits Kate. 'They styled me. It was completely contrived, you know; hunch over, whatever. The pictures were about fashion, not documentary.'

After meeting Corinne and Melanie, Kate 'upgraded from jumble sales to Portobello Market and that's when you start throwing things together like that'.

'Second-hand clothes were a very critical thing for them,' says fashion designer Liza Bruce, who would work with the three women in the early 1990s. 'The thing about thrift stores is that you see everything jumbled up together, and it's that juxtaposition [that is so inspiring]; you see the things that are hidden, that jump out at you, those are very stimulating things.' Like a child's flick-book where a policeman is suddenly wearing a ballet tutu and cowboy boots, the chaotic kaleidoscope of the market stalls was helping Kate absorb unusual combinations of clothes.

'Our look then was an eclectic mix,' recalls Ward, 'vintage bias-cut 1930s dresses worn with trainers, cashmere sweaters with holes in the elbows, raw-cut boyfriend pants; falling off us and draping on the ground.'

Ward claims the key to this new fashion formula was 'all about irreverence and exaggerated proportions: mini and maxi, super-skinny, extra-long sleeves, pants hanging off our hipbones and dragging on the floor, vests with skinny straps and shrunken waistcoats': a subversive play on the balance of clothing, and an instant education in styling for Kate.

'It wasn't about [new] designer clothes in those days because they weren't really making things that we wanted to wear,' says Ward. But at that time, Portobello Market had treasure of its own: 'There was tons of Biba lying around then,' says *Cheap Date* editor Kira Joliffe, who was assisting another of Ward's contemporaries, stylist Venetia Scott, 'and old designer clothes like [1960s fashion legend] Ossie Clark, and it felt like only three people in the world had heard of him. It didn't occur to me it could be collectible one day; you just didn't see clothes in those terms. And it was never called "vintage"; vintage was 1920s, or like, a vintage car. It was just "second hand".'

And because the clothes were easy come, easy go, the girls developed a carefree attitude to grooming and finish, and a healthy disrespect and spontaneity towards the clothes. 'We weren't afraid to just chop at things with scissors,' says Ward, referring to their endless attempts at customising; rolling up skirts, and simply cutting off hems to shorten dresses. 'Our look was always effortless, a little bit "she's come undone". There were no boundaries between day and night or expensive and cheap. In a way we completely redefined a new sophistication.'

There was only one unspoken rule that all the Portobello girls adhered to. Perhaps the most important lesson that Kate learned from her stylist friends and their contemporaries was that the coolest looking people were always wearing the most authentic clothes.

Back then, the Portobello Market was still the haunt of neighbourhood faces; a multicultural melting pot of older residents and newer arrivals, impoverished students, struggling musicians and down-at-heel trust-fund kids, trawling the markets for fashion relics bought dirt-cheap from their favourite sellers.

'I remember getting things like a multicoloured patchwork suede waistcoat with fringing from the 1970s,' says Joliffe, 'or a Harris tweed riding jacket would be a real find, or a beautiful 1940s black gabardine skirt suit, all for like, seriously, a fiver.' And the quirkier, the better: 'We were always jumping on ostrich feather boas or something weird and interesting; like a genuine circus performer's leotard with sparkly bits.'

Kate got that it was cooler to be the real deal; to be the girl in the original 1970s tour band T-shirt, found screwed up in a cardboard box of stuff on a stall (still with mysterious cigarette burn on the chest); that a great wardrobe didn't need to cost a fortune, but it did need to be hunted down, and that finding great clothes takes a bit of effort (maybe getting up early on Fridays to trawl the market with a milky coffee and a custard tart from the Portuguese Lisboa café), a bit of knowledge (like knowing that the best shoes – kitten-heel mesh slingbacks from the 1950s, or original Biba suede go-go boots – came from the girl with the stall under the railway bridge) and a bit of luck (like when, to the other girls' rage, Kate pulled out a perfectly slouchy men's pinstriped trouser suit that she loved and wore for years).

None of her new friends shopped on the high street. One time Corinne bought a pair of black PVC jeans from a Soho sex shop for £25 which she wore with a polo neck and old school trainers. But none of them wanted to look like they were trying to follow fashion trends. And despite the hours they spent roaming the market, nobody wanted to look like they were trying too hard.

Soon, James Brown moved in with Corinne Day in central London. Kate was constantly hanging out there too. Still a reportage photographer at heart, Corinne never stopped taking pictures of her, and Kate grew more and more relaxed in front of the camera. 'Nobody tells you what to do,' she says, 'and that was quite good because that's why I was natural. I was just like a normal teenager.'

But John Galliano got her. As Storm became more high profile, Kate was sent to Paris on castings, where for spring/summer 1990, Galliano, a highly respected young designer from London, was showing for the first time. Kate was appearing on the catwalk with the Amazonian supermodels Naomi Campbell, Linda Evangelista and Christy Turlington. Tiny and pale in a simple black sleeveless dress, Kate opened the show. The designer called her his 'Lolita'.

Kate was so petrified before the show that she couldn't eat all day. 'I had to come down the catwalk by myself. It looked huge, like an airport runway – I was so nervous. The runway was the longest one I've ever seen. I felt like it went on forever and I was up there on my own.'

Afterwards, everyone sat in the designer's office, watching the video footage of the show. Kate got drunk on whisky and later passed out at the post-show dinner, missing her flight home the next day. 'I was supposed to be back at school on Monday morning, and I was still in Paris on Wednesday.'

Perhaps not surprisingly, 'during that time I kind of lost interest in school'. Kate pretty much moved in with Corinne from the ages of fifteen to seventeen: 'I ended up living with her for a while

Talking backstage
with a male
friend at a Paris
fashion show, 1991.

and we'd just end up hanging out all the time. And talk about fashion and what we were going to do and draw pictures. She had very strong opinions and very strong ideas about what she wanted to do.'

Liza Bruce claims the girls' shared suburban backgrounds 'had a lot to do with the intensity of their friendship. With them, to get to New York was the pinnacle. They wanted to prove themselves. They wanted to get those advertising campaigns.' She recalls that Corinne in particular was ferociously focused: 'Corinne was like, "I'm getting us into *Vogue*". But back then, [for unknown outsiders] *i-D* maybe, but never *Vogue*, but Corinne had her sights set on that … they wouldn't have had that ambition [without her],' insists Bruce. 'She had this almost witch-like quality: "If I say it's going to happen … I have decided."'

One freezing cold spring morning in 1989, Corinne, Melanie and Kate headed to a windswept beach in the out-of-season seaside town of Camber Sands, in East Sussex. The shoot would change the course of fashion photography forever. Kate appeared topless in a miniskirt and fancy dress Native American headdress; Melanie added a daisy chain over a simple white smock; Kate shivered naked with just a straw Stetson covering her skinny modesty. Corinne shot the black and white images with her usual intimate realism.

James did Kate's hair, barely touching it, but for adding two tiny plaits. 'We ended up working together professionally for the first time on the Corinne Day shoot for *The Face*,' says James. 'It was a big deal for both of us, but doing her hair had just the same vibe as when we were back in Croydon. We'd talk, have a laugh and things would just happen.'

What happened was that Kate became the face of a generation. *The Face* published the shoot a year later in its July 1990 issue. Kate appeared on the cover in the Indian headdress, giggling and barefaced and freckly, flashing pointy crooked teeth under the headline 'The 3rd Summer of Love'. She looked as she was: a skint, carefree teenager, having a laugh.

'It was a story that was talked about and that people related to,' says Kate. 'It captured what was going on in England at the time.' At the time, as *The Face* reported in the same issue, rave culture was reaching its peak, with teenagers dancing all night in decrepit abandoned warehouses. 'It wasn't 1980s glamour. It was about the street,' says Kate. 'Everyone was saying, "Let's get off our tits and have a laugh. Be more real and not have to grow

up so quickly. And have fun."'

The girls spent most of 1990 shooting for *The Face*, bringing with them a whole new approach to photography and fashion, Kate acknowledges. 'I think [Corinne] did succeed in changing things a bit.'

Their inspirations were diverse and often dark. Hairstylist Michael Boadi, who would later work with Kate on many of her most high-profile editorial shoots, recalls that at that time 'There was a German film that Corinne took all these [style] references from, Christiane F [a 1981 German documentary about teenage heroine addicts in Berlin] … that was their thing; they wanted to live that whole look; without the drugs of course.'

Even after the success and recognition from *The Face* cover, the girls continued to be obsessed with second-hand clothes. In 1990, fashion writer Melanie Rickey was working at Rocket, grading second-hand clothes 'in a big old dusty warehouse off a street in Crouch End and Melanie Ward used to come to in looking for things. And then one day she brought Kate there to do a shoot, surrounded by all the bales of clothes.' The 'Summer of Love' *Face* cover had just been published. 'Kate must have only been sixteen at the time, but she was so incandescently beautiful you got the feeling you were around someone amazing; you couldn't stop looking at her.'

Mario Sorrenti describes his first sighting of Kate as 'an aesthetic shock. She was the most beautiful woman I've ever seen.' An Italian-born New Yorker, Mario had been modelling for years and had recently starred in a Levi's commercial set in a pool hall. Like Corinne, he was making the transition to photography. From a family of photographers, he had begun documenting his own life in pictures since his teens, and in 1990 started taking photographs of his fellow models hanging around on castings and backstage at the shows.

Before long, he bumped into Kate, who had started seeing a friend of his. '[Mario] said he wanted to take pictures of me,' says Kate. 'He got my phone number and rang me up to say he wanted to make me a model. That was funny … We were together and we would do pictures as well, because he wanted to be a photographer.'

Mario became the second fly-on-the-wall in Kate's life. 'I took endless shots of her when we were together … and even now I never get tired of photographing her.'

Soon the twenty-year-old Sorrenti showed

these photographic diaries to Phil Bicker at *The Face*, which led to a spread for the magazine with a freelance stylist, Camilla Nickerson. Within a few months, his work was popping up everywhere.

The pair lived together at Kate's mum's house before moving to London some months later, renting a room in fashion photographer Marc Lebon's colourful house in West London.

Kate's fashion education was starting to move beyond clothes. 'If you're in with photographers, they show you photographic books,' says Liza Bruce. 'They'll say, "We want to do the picture like this."'

'Most things are referenced, aren't they?' Kate would say nonchalantly, years later. 'And because I'd been out with a photographer, we'd look at books all the time, so I did know a lot of images. Fashion, you know.'

During this time, Kate developed 'a passion for images'. Mario says, 'I think that was partly why she loved modelling. We were inspired by iconic images tremendously, and that influenced the way we wished to see ourselves. I think as she grew up so did her understanding of images and of herself and her sense of style.'

'The thing that most people don't understand about modelling is that it's not just being pushed up against the wall,' says Bruce. 'You have to give a huge amount of energy. It is immensely exhausting and hard work. Kate really has that determination. To do that well you have to have looked at a lot of history, a lot of fashion and a lot of pictures to immediately get what a photographer wants.'

Travel was broadening their minds too; the girls took a trip to Borneo for a swimwear shoot for *The Face* in 1991, with Kate photographed on the beach barefaced and freckly, with wet salty hair. Corinne recalls, 'In Borneo we saw little girls dressed in party dresses and flip-flops. Everything is out of context.' This mismatching was a key part of the girls' look; boots with slip dresses, a man's suit with trainers. The multicultural mix of their Notting Hill neighbourhood was another inspiration. 'In London you'll see the most beautiful Indian woman wearing the most exquisite silk sari,' says Melanie, 'and she's got on a pair of boots, but for functional reasons – to go shopping in the rain. I love it when people wear things for functional reasons.'

This look was happening on the other side of the world too. After the summer music festivals in 1991, Nirvana released the seminal album Nevermind, and grunge exploded across America. Suddenly kids were wearing a rough-and-tumble mix of thrift-store clothes and workwear, plaid shirts and ripped baggy jeans. Girls wore loose, layered clothes: long-sleeved T-shirts, with long button-through dresses and heavy boots.

At this time, no designer reacted more quickly to changes in the current zeitgeist than Calvin Klein. Aware that his teenage daughter represented a new generation of customers who couldn't relate to his label's polished catwalk glamour, the designer was looking for a new, younger image.

Kate had flown to New York with Mario, who was showing his photography book to various magazines. Kate was sent on a casting to meet influential art director Fabien Baron at *Harper's Bazaar* magazine. Baron knew that Calvin Klein had recently wanted to cast the elfin French model and singer Vanessa Paradis for an advertising campaign, but the contract had fallen through.

'And then I brought him Kate Moss,' Baron says. 'I made her come in one afternoon and try on a jean.' Klein took one look and hired Kate instantly. 'Calvin fell in love with her.'

British model Angela Dunn was at the Calvin Klein offices the same afternoon. 'We were all waiting in reception and everyone walking out of the room was saying, "She's so gorgeous, so beautiful, have you ever seen anyone like her?" We could hear people whispering, "She looks amazing in everything that she puts on!" The stylist would walk out, and then Calvin Klein's PA; there was a big scene going on. I'll never forget it, and another model and I were looking at each other and saying, "Who is going to come out of that room?"

'And then, of course, forty-five minutes later, she emerges, in a long skirt, flat shoes and a polo neck, really understated, typical Kate.'

Dunn had encountered Kate on the model circuit: 'I knew who she was; there was already a buzz about her. She walked out, and was all sweet and natural and just said, "Hello!"'

But Melanie understood what Calvin saw in the young Londoner. 'Kate was never, and will never be, a fashion victim. She always looks cool, sexy and modern. She wears her clothes; they never wear her. No amount of money can buy style – you either have it or you don't. Kate definitely has it.'

The most high-profile fashion designer on the planet was buying into Kate's look. And she was still only seventeen.

# 3

## The London Look

'Most of the designers weren't doing
things I wanted anyway. I still
had to go to second-hand shops.'
KATE MOSS

Paris, 1993.

here's a difference between clothing and fashion. As Kate already knew, any lowly piece of second-hand clothing can look cool, but high fashion is a different thing altogether, and Kate was about to encounter it properly for the first time.

Dolce & Gabbana had chosen Kate as one of the faces of their autumn/winter 1992 campaign. 'It was absolutely Kate's first major job,' says the shoot's stylist, Lori Goldstein, 'and her first foray into modelling, because previously her shoots were just about her, just about a girl.'

The shoot took place in a vast vacant studio in a warehouse off New York's West-side highway. 'It was a big production, even for Dolce & Gabbana; there was a wardrobe area, lights, scenery,' recalls Goldstein. And there was top photographer Steven Meisel, 'and this was a period when he had shot all these girls who went on to become supermodels'.

Meisel was the star-maker; a svengali figure who could transform models with the kind of advice on hairstyles or posing more usually associated with the movie studios of the 1940s. It was Meisel who taught the supreme super, Linda Evangelista, to adopt her dazzling, Monroe-esque open-mouthed smile, and Meisel who had her raise a haughty arched eyebrow that gave her a feline femininity. And it was Meisel who would persuade Linda's hairstylist Garren to switch the colour of her famous crop from brunette to blonde to paprika red during a single season of catwalk shows.

It was the height of supermodel-mania. Linda had famously joked that she and Christy

Opposite page: With
Christy Turlington at
a Ralph Lauren
fashion show, 1993.

'The silver dress was the same as one stylist Melanie Ward
had  originally asked me to make, based on a vintage piece,
a gold antique dress she had found; she wasn't interested in
the dress, but she did like the fabric.
And then [photographer] Corinne [Day] wanted to do a
shoot and asked me to do it in silver, the dress Melanie
had previously asked for in gold.
So this was Corinne's dress. Kate and Corinne were like
girlfriends, living together, "Can I borrow your jacket?" "Can
I borrow your dress?". After an *i-D* shoot with Kate wearing the
gold dress, I made this for Corinne, and she photographed it
on Linda Evangelista for British *Vogue*, and then Kate wore it to
the party.  Eventually I got the dress back, so I guess it was on
loan. The pants came with the dress. They were a very heavy fabric,
crepe lycra, rather primitive. Not nice and slinky, it was heavy,
almost 1930s stuff. It was a juxtaposition, the light slip,
the chunky pants; so boyish. It wasn't sexy underwear. "Underwear
as outerwear", that was the mood of the moment.
The dress did come out more transparent in the picture,
it is woven metallic fabric, but dense. So it wouldn't have
looked so transparent in reality, which is maybe why she
had the confidence to wear it.
But it was sheer. I think she was comfortable with it, I don't
think she thought about it at all. It was transparent, and she was
so utterly comfortable with that idea. It wasn't a come on,
and "How fabulously sexy am I?", it was just, "This is me".
And she looked so sweet. Her body language was so
much like a kid's. You can see by her make up and
her hair; completely like a boy; pulled back, no make up.'
LIZA BRUCE, FASHION DESIGNER, LONDON

Kate with Naomi Campbell and Linda Evangelista.

Turlington 'won't wake up for less than $10,000 a day' and along with Naomi Campbell they were The Trinity, an elite group of models who, alongside Cindy Crawford and Tatiana Patitz, had become the darlings of the catwalks, commanding $50,000 a show, appearing on countless *Vogue* covers and beyond; lip-synching George Michael's song 'Freedom! '90' for his music video. (A subsequent repeat performance on Gianni Versace's catwalk brought the house down.)

The supermodels all had emphatically individual looks, linked only by awe-inspiring bone structures, Barbie bodies, and the unblinking gaze of total self-assurance in their own beauty, verging on vanity.

And then there was Kate. 'When I first met her she was no more than a child,' says Manolo Blahnik. 'She was too short, too skinny, her teeth weren't perfect … she was the complete opposite of what the term "supermodel" meant at the time.'

Yet even beside a young Tyra Banks, and Nadja Auermann, a glamazonian German with a 45" inner seam, Kate stood out: 'She had such an innocent and young face,' says Domenico Dolce, recalling his favourite shot from the campaign, with Kate 'framed by a feather boa … an extraordinary beauty that couldn't go unnoticed'. Stefano Gabbana says, 'The first supermodels were very tall and curvy, but Kate just looked so young and innocent. This made her stand out among the other models.'

The collection, called 'The Trip', was inspired

by the 1970s: patchwork and velvet, flares and floppy hats. 'It was glamorous; total high fashion,' recalls Goldstein. 'Totally rock and roll too. I don't even know if Kate knew at that stage that this was what she was going to become; it was very Keith Richards and very cool,'

Kate was already well aware of that era and all it stood for. 'I like the 1970s, but I don't see myself as a hippie; I wasn't born 'til 1974!' But she was a fan of 'Janis Joplin, flares and having a good time. There was no Aids, everyone slept around and there were lots of drugs.' She was listening to Hendrix and Bowie, as well as Primal Scream and Paul Weller.

'She was actually quite shy then; she [still] is a little bit,' says Lori Goldstein, 'not like an Agyness [Deyn] who walks in and you get how obsessed she is with fashion. You didn't see Kate's style then; it grew as she became more confident in this business.' But something had happened to Kate. 'Through this first experience she probably became conscious that fashion was what she desired,' says Stefano Gabbana.

Back home, hairstylist Michael Boadi, then also starting out, recalls bumping into Kate in the West London neighbourhood where they both lived. The Meisel shoot had made quite an impression. 'She was like, "I did the Dolce campaign, and there was this genius pair of shoes and I'm gonna get them, and I'm going to put them with this and that…" And that's how it started; that's when the [designer] labels kicked in. That's when she started

getting into dressing up; proper fashion clothing.'

Kate already had high-fashion eyebrows to go with her new look; they had been plucked into oblivion on her first shoot for *Harper's Bazaar* with photographer Steven Klein. They would take months to grow back.

But first, there was Calvin.

The ad campaign, photographed by Patrick Demarchelier for Calvin Klein Jeans, debuted in September. Kate became a fashion phenomenon overnight. 'I was on every bus!' As with the *Face* cover, 'Kate became an icon for a new generation,' says Melanie.

Kate, wearing white Calvin Klein briefs with a logo-ed waistband and little else, was draped across the muscular bare chest of baggy-jeans-clad rapper Marky Mark Wahlberg. With her fine-arched brows, smoky eyes and Clara Bow pout, Kate resembled an ingénue starlet from the 1920s.

'It's a new kind of beauty,' said Calvin Klein at the time. 'Not the big, sporty, superwoman type, but glamour, which is more sensitive, more fragile.' But this fragility sparked a storm of controversy, and the images were condemned by eating disorder experts. Kate's posters were scrawled with graffiti reading, 'Feed me'.

'Calvin fearlessly embraced what we were doing in fashion and photography,' says Melanie, 'and the new idea of beauty as exemplified by Kate.'

Kate and Marky Mark also launched a new, younger jeans line: CK Calvin Klein. 'I remember completely reworking black jeans for Kate to wear

in the advertising campaign to give them attitude,' says Melanie, who Calvin had hired to work on the line, 'stapling them up the back, lowering the crotch to make them into hipsters. I also sanded them and greased them to make them look lived-in and personal to Kate. Strangely enough, black was quite un-cool then and nobody was making pants and jeans that sat on the hip.' Afterwards, Kate would always approach jeans as a statement piece, frequently choosing cutting edge styles, before anyone else was wearing them.

When Kate arrived at the shows in Milan, it looked like a clash of generations. Everything that had gone before, from the supermodels' stylised outfits, to their overly made-up glamour-grooming and showy logo-laden accessories, suddenly looked fake and dated. By then, Linda and Christy had already been modelling for the best part of a decade. Kate, with her cocky, slung-together style and sweetly fresh-faced English-schoolgirl looks, could have been one of the supermodels' daughters.

'I remember when I went to the shows, people looked at me funny,' says Kate, but she wasn't craving flashy designer labels. 'I never thought I was going to make as much money as them anyway.'

Kate's entire wardrobe probably didn't add up to the price of a Chanel handbag. Her second-hand clothes made her stand out in a sea of label-smothered supermodels wearing gaudy Versace printed silk shirts (Linda), brightly coloured

With Mario
Sorrenti in 1993.

Chanel jackets (Naomi) and Azzedine Alaia stretchy Lycra miniskirts (Cindy). They arrived in limos, flew Concorde and had superstar boyfriends (Cindy was Mrs Richard Gere and Naomi was dating U2's Adam Clayton).

'I couldn't really relate to anyone just because they were so fashiony,' says Kate, 'and I was from Croydon, and I was like, "What are these people talking about?"'

At that time, despite being constantly surrounded by high-end fashion, the look backstage was not particularly cutting edge. 'The other models didn't have a clue,' says ex-model and former MTV stylist John Bland. 'The other girls were walking round in, like, MaxMara.' Or, as Kate recalls, 'The model uniform – everyone wore jeans and a boot.'

By contrast, Kate's look was still very much 'poor girl' glamour. She wore too-long skirts or baggy trousers, with simple vest tops or T-shirts and trainers. For evening, she favoured antique silk nightgowns worn with high-heeled suede boots.

'Kate loved feeling very sexy and seductive, but it was in her own way,' says Mario. 'It was a mixture of street style and sexy elegance. Those were the things that came naturally to her. She always needed to be true to her self – that's what made her feel comfortable. She never needed to try very hard.'

'I remember looking out the window of a taxi in Paris, and noticing this incredibly pretty girl *Opposite page: Paris, 1993* walking down the street,' says Bella Freud. 'She was in boyish trousers that were too long and dragging on the ground and plimsolls and a T-shirt. And this incredibly handsome boy was with her, and he was brushing aside her hair, off the face of this gorgeous girl, and it was Kate and Mario. It could have been on a street anywhere in the world; they just looked like a couple of kids.'

Kate was intimidated by the supers. 'I looked up to Christy [Turlington], and was in awe of her. And once, when I had to get changed in front of Linda Evangelista, I was scared because I felt so little compared to her.'

'Kate's always been tiny,' says Bella Freud. 'The supermodels literally were really tall.'

But soon it was, 'Naomi, Linda, Christy, with the new girl,' says Lori. 'That kind of happens in this business. It's like school; "Do we like her? Don't we?" Naomi has a very nurturing side.'

'When I met Naomi and Christy they took me under their wing; we had so much fun that first season,' remembers Kate, 'staying between Christy and Naomi's rooms, and it was all limos and the Ritz Hotel and all that kind of business. It was Versace, and parties; every night there was something you had to go to – and then you had to be up at six. I mean, it was fun!'

And Kate was the perfect clothes horse. 'I remember seeing her at an early CK fashion show and thinking she was remarkably flat,' says Liza Bruce, 'like a piece of paper, really astonishing. Of course [models] can be skinny, but this was

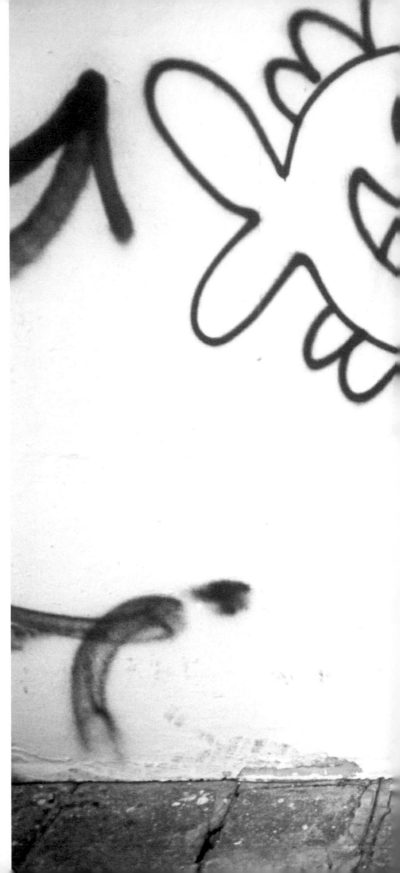

very particular, she was like … a slice. But from another side she had curves. She's not a boy. She's an amalgam of woman and boy; her breasts are childlike, but then the hips are womanly – she is super-curvaceous in a bikini. She's got an extraordinary body; she doesn't have long legs but then she's got these hips.'

Kate's un-supermodel-like proportions presented problems. Designer Julien Macdonald first met Kate when he was working behind the scenes at Chanel. 'Karl was making her special shoes, because she's so tiny [Kate has size 36 feet]. Backstage it was always "Where are Kate's shoes?" He had to put a wedge in, special shoes, so she was as high as the other girls. And there was always a special Kate outfit; smaller than all the other outfits.'

Kate was making her presence felt on the catwalks. 'She's always had this ability to be so elegant,' says Bella Freud. 'She can just work it, and when she starts, it just dazzles. It's just incredible for a model, completely indefinable, and she can do it more than anybody. She gets in there. She was so tiny, but she was incredible … like a cartoon.'

'Kate is more of an actress than a model,' says Stefano Gabbana. 'She is able to interpret many kinds of woman. She was on the catwalks of many of our fashion shows throughout the 1990s.'

'I remember when she started doing Yves Saint Laurent,' says Bella Freud. 'Loulou de la Falaise [Saint Laurent's muse] was flipping out about her, saying, "She's incredible!" talking about her just having this gracefulness.'

'Kate wore the cream slip dress, before she really got into "vintage", as I call it. And she was one of the first to do it, you know. Although I had been wearing those sorts of dresses in the shop for years. Back in those days she was really friendly with models Naomi, and Susie Bick and Helena Christensen, and they all really were the first to do it...
It looked quite unusual at the time. Now you can buy little slips from Topshop obviously, or Oasis or wherever, but nobody else was doing it back then.
It was quite outrageous really, to wear those slips and the little cami-knickers as outerwear, and... wear them with a little skinny cardigan or a little beaded cape. We forget that now, but it is interesting because it was quite outrageous at the time. Quite revolutionary.'

VIRGINIA BATES,
VIRGINIA VINTAGE CLOTHING, LONDON

Kate had achieved the impossible; the chain-smoking mousey-haired schoolgirl with the anti-fashion wardrobe was conquering the catwalks, infiltrating the elite ranks of the supermodels, and all without losing her sense of self. 'She was just this little thing; she was very urchin-like,' says Freud, 'and then she had this punkish attitude of going into this grand world and making her way.'

In Paris, Kate easily fell in with the group of ex-pats who had staged a British invasion of the French capital over the past decade. John Galliano and Vivienne Westwood had moved their catwalk shows across the Channel, and were playing up their patriotism, making it seem cool to be British. Galliano sent Kate down the catwalk in a tiny Union Flag blazer, which she kept afterwards. Naomi might have been a fellow Londoner, but Kate was the new Brit on the block.

The shows moved on to New York. 'Kate was there, and she had already done the [Calvin Klein] jeans campaign, and there was this huge energy,' remembers Liza Bruce. 'She started to be photographed by paparazzi. Corinne, Melanie and Kate had been out to a club and realised "Oh my goodness – this is an avalanche".'

Marc Jacobs, then designer at Perry Ellis, had been fascinated with the girls' 'undone' styling since the 1990 *Face* cover. And when he called Kate in for a pre-show fitting, he was completely enchanted by her hand-me-down personal style. 'She walked in wearing these Adidas trainers and a Martin Margiela skirt that was miles too long, but she'd just rolled it up to fit.'

Jacobs recalls thinking 'that attitude towards clothes is exactly what's needed now'. Jacobs' controversial grunge collection that season, all plaid shirts, knitted beanie hats and long floral dresses, took the fashion world by storm, resulting in his immediate sacking from the American sportswear label, but ultimately making the designer's name.

'Kate's look really reflects what has gone on in the music world and that has influenced fashion,' designer Anna Sui told *The Face* that year. 'The spirit is less "look at me, look at me". The same has happened with clothes, and it's now far less "look how much I've spent".'

Kate spent her time 'shopping – a lot!' but the photos show her in Parisian flea markets, rather than upmarket boutiques, and she admits, 'I don't buy loads.'

Within a year, the ever-savvy chief super-model Linda Evangelista would shed her high-gloss, groomed-to-perfection image and reinvent herself for the grunge era; make-up-less with rootsy bleached hair, modelling very-Kate men's-style trouser suits and slip dresses for a Corinne Day shoot for British *Vogue*. Soon the sexy 1980s excess of Gianni Versace would make way for the edgy minimalism of Prada and Helmut Lang.

In January 1993, Melanie, Kate and Corinne were featured in *Interview* magazine, which declared that they were 'about to conquer an America hungry for a new look'. The accompanying portrait showed the girls looking like sisters; defiantly pouty, with long, lank, centre-parted hair in skin-tight black clothing. Melanie and Corinne were interviewed, by now finishing each other's sentences.

They set out their vintage manifesto: 'We're not inspired by things that are retro for retro's sake,' says Melanie. 'You have to take things from the past and make them into the present,' continues Corinne. 'Just because you've got a 1960s top doesn't mean you have to put on a pair of platforms and false eyelashes.'

Kate's vintage tastes were edging upmarket, with a little help from some of the best vintage dealers in the business. In 1992 Mark Steinberg and Tracey Tolkien opened their legendary Kings Road vintage store Steinberg & Tolkien. Pricier than Portobello Market, and the charmingly jumbled Cornucopia, Steinberg's was Kate's introduction to upscale collectible vintage.

'I can remember her coming in right in the beginning,' says Tracey Tolkien. 'Kate always made vintage look so good, because her taste is so good. She made vintage look modern. Some people would wear vintage and make it look terrible and tatty and like it just came out of the dressing-up box. With Kate, it looked more modern than the new stuff. And certainly more edgy.'

'The whole point about vintage is you have to know what suits you,' says Tolkien. 'Kate was so unflinching in being able to just pick stuff. And she had the most eclectic taste of all of our customers. Some people would only just buy tea dresses, or slip dresses. With her, the experimentation was relentless; she was always changing.'

'The real beauty about being a model is that you get to put on clothes,' says Liza Bruce, 'and when you put on clothes, on and off and on and off and on and off, then you have this wonderful ability to just pick up clothes. Clothes have this power, but playing with clothes to such a degree liberates you from that. So that you suddenly have a "third eye", you have another vision that you just don't get from walking into a store, trying a couple of things on, shopping. You're seeing how you play with clothes. Clothes which you would never necessarily choose to try on yourself. You're playing a game that adds to your own [style] vocabulary.'

Even when Kate could afford to buy modern labels, she preferred to buy vintage. 'Most of the designers weren't doing things I wanted anyway. I still had to go to second-hand shops.'

Since appearing in his show, Kate had started obsessively collecting John Galliano's designs. 'She used to buy loads of early Galliano,' says Tracey Tolkien, 'and he was trying to buy it back too! It was produced in such small quantities, because from his first show he had no money. But those two were the first to buy back his stuff.' Kate would hunt out beautifully cut but quirky pieces like the asymmetric jackets with one sleeve longer than the other that appeared off-centre.

Asked in an *i-D* interview if there was anything she wouldn't do in a photoshoot, Kate answers, 'I wouldn't wear fur, but you don't get asked to do that so much any more.' And so she must have been passing over the many fur coats, capes and stoles she would have seen in all the vintage stores and Parisian flea markets.

The following year, animal rights group PETA would launch its infamous 'I'd Rather Go Naked than Wear Fur' campaign, featuring a line-up of nude supermodels including Christy, Cindy and Naomi.

In January, after just four short years, Kate and Corinne had achieved their ultimate ambition; to work together for *Vogue*. Corinne shot Kate for her first cover for British *Vogue* in March 1993. James Brown did her hair, simply scraping it back off the face to reveal her elfin features. 'I wanted Kate to look like Kate,' he said, referring to the natural look that was already becoming his (and Kate's) signature style.

The head-and-shoulders shot, revealing little more than the straps of a pastel-flecked white Chanel shift dress, focused in on Kate's kittenish face; bare, but for the merest hint of mascara and lip-gloss and a smattering of freckles. Across her chest was the headline 'London Style, London Girls – Fashion's New Spirit'.

But before that issue had even hit the news stands, another set of photographs of Kate arrived in *Vogue*'s Art Department, which proved to be the most controversial in the magazine's 77-year history, and would ultimately rip apart the girls' friendship for the rest of the decade.

The shoot, entitled 'Under-exposure', had been shot by Corinne in Kate and Mario's own West London flat; in the room they rented from photographer Marc Lebon. The flat, a bit messy, a bit squalid, with make-do furniture, a nylon quilt and fairy lights taped to the wall, was an average-looking rental flat, but jarred uncomfortably with the high-gloss images in *Vogue*. Kate looked skinny and a bit vacant in cheap synthetic knickers, flimsy T-shirts and vests and ill-fitting bras.

When the issue went on sale, the pictures caused an uproar. *Vogue* was accused of promoting child porn. 'It was upsetting sometimes,' says Kate of the reaction, 'but I was really young and skinny and some girls just are. That was me; I wasn't trying to be anyone else.'

But the controversy ultimately destroyed the girls' friendship. 'Melanie and I went our separate ways,' says Corinne. 'She thought I took my work too personally; she was right, I did. Melanie moved to America and never spoke to me again. My friendship with Kate also ended around the same time.'

Corinne later claimed to have had a revelation while taking the photographs of Kate. 'Halfway through the *Vogue* shoot I realised it wasn't fun for her any more, and that she was no longer my best friend but had become a "model". She hadn't realised how beautiful she was, and when she did, I found I didn't think her beautiful any more.'

'I was there and witnessed the whole thing,' says Liza Bruce. 'It was a friendship that was so intense, that deep. And then all these jealousies kicked in … and it got really weird.'

Kate's grungy appearances in the media contrasted sharply with her increasingly lavish lifestyle. She and Mario, who had been living at home with his family in their apartment in Manhattan, suddenly found themselves jet-set and homeless.

'The adventure was really rock 'n' roll,' recalls Mario. 'Suddenly we were living in luxury hotels in Berlin, London, New York, Paris; so much so that we ended up giving up the apartment and living exclusively in hotels.' Kate's schedule was gruelling; sometimes taking up to three transatlantic flights in a single week.

In the space of just a year, Kate had been photographed by most of the world's top photographers; from Bruce Weber to Herb Ritts and Patrick Demarchelier, Helmut Newton, Steven Meisel and Richard Avedon.

'It was an incredible period,' says Mario. 'I went from having nothing to a contract for Harper's Bazaar, and working with Kate for the Calvin Klein Obsession campaign.'

'WHEN YOU THINK ABOUT IT, KATE MOSS STARTED OFF AS A BIT OF AN ODDITY... AND YET IN SPITE OF IT ALL, SHE SUCCEEDED TO BECOME THE MOST INFLUENTIAL AND POWERFUL MODEL OF HER TIME, GOING ON TO BECOME THIS BEAUTIFUL WOMAN – ONE WHO HAS THE POWER TO MAKE MILLIONS OF WOMEN ALL OVER THE WORLD WANT WHAT SHE WEARS SO EFFORTLESSLY. AND I KNOW THAT BECAUSE EVEN FIFTEEN YEARS AFTER SHE FIRST WORE THEM, PEOPLE STILL COME TO THE SHOP ASKING FOR THE "KATE MOSS MARY JANES" - WHICH SHE STILL WEARS TODAY!'

Manolo Blahnik

Premiere of
Philadelphia,
December 1993.

'I've tried and I've tried but I just can't get out of my Adidas trainers.'

KATE MOSS

Earlier that summer, 'Calvin Klein had seen personal photos of Kate that I had shot on vacation with her, and he thought they were great. His request was that I do the same for his campaign, so he sent us both to an island on our own for ten days.'

They rented a beautiful beach house. 'We had the worst time,' says Kate. 'We fought the whole time.' But the resulting images, black and white grainy photographs and shaky video footage of a naked Kate, bathing in the sea, were perfect for the perfume's television ads and print campaign. 'Obsession is a good word to describe our relationship,' says Mario. 'Calvin was very clever; he saw that.'

The advert's soundtrack – Mario breathily declaring, 'I love you. I love you, Kate.' – was his idea, recorded on a whim, as a confused Kate overheard from the room next door. 'Because we were going out, it was such a personal thing that became public. I suppose that was a turning point. We were just on holiday. I love those pictures.'

Mario also shot Kate for the Obsession for Men campaign, lying naked front-down on a sofa. 'He always wanted me to take my clothes off,' said Kate, 'and I didn't really feel comfortable with it a lot of the time because I didn't think it was necessary. But he used to be so obsessed with, like, it had to be a pure picture, so y'know that was his vision, and he is the artist.'

Kate's self-consciousness was possibly heightened by the fact that the photos were shot outdoors, on a rooftop high above the Urban Outfitters store on Broadway, overlooked by the office workers and

residents of the surrounding skyscrapers.

The Obsession campaigns debuted in the autumn. But after months of working in different time-zones, 'We split up soon after that,' says Kate. 'I would be sitting at home late at night on the phone with the TV on and [the Obsession ad would appear] I'd be like "Oops".'

Although Kate was now single, little did she know that Calvin Klein would have a hand in her next relationship. 'I was doing pictures for Calvin Klein and the photographer had stacks of pictures of Johnny [Depp]. He wanted the style of the advertising to be like the pictures of Johnny. There was Johnny everywhere. And this photographer was, like, all the time: "Find me a girl, find me a girl." And I said, "Introduce me to Johnny and I'll find you a girlfriend." So I had all these pictures in the house months before we ever met.'

Kate had lost both Mario and Corinne, but their impact on her professionally had been invaluable.

'I think Kate was lucky enough from a very young age to work with the most amazing photographers,' says stylist Brana Wolf. 'Mario is really an artist. He gave her a love affair with the camera so that she would understand that photography had all these layers. She got good at becoming great characters. While Mario photographed her in one way, Steven Meisel would do something totally different.'

'The nice thing about being a model is that they do educate you,' says Liza Bruce. 'You're with very sophisticated people; stylists, photographers, art directors, and they all have access to other worlds and they tap into a lot of things, like architecture or art.'

And Kate was absorbing it all. 'Not everyone would get the same thing from that situation,' says Bruce. 'I think you have to have some kind of natural ability to absorb that. Kate has an inherent ability to learn; she's very smart, so she's very astute.'

So Kate was already an undergraduate of the world's most exclusive fashion finishing school.

By the next season of shows she was also gaining confidence on the catwalk. 'I thought, "If I can do the runway with all these taller girls, then nothing can stand in my way."'

The Galliano show remained her favourite. 'It was amazing, like a high – the adrenaline, and "You're on, and you're going to be this and do that!" John tells you your character and you just get so into it because of the energy.'

Galliano's collection that season was 'partly inspired by Princess Anastasia's escape from Russia,' he recalls. 'Kate wore this magnificent pale blue striped crinoline skirt, with talc in her hair. In passing, I had simply said to her, "OK, Kate, you are being pursued by wolves." And she played it from the heart. She ran flat out. Nobody had ever seen a crinoline flying like that on the catwalk! It was completely disrespectful. And everyone rose. It was a magic moment.'

After the show, Galliano let Kate keep the Mary Janes (a high-heeled shoe with a single strap fastening across the foot) designed by Manolo Blahnik for the show. Kate quickly became a Blahnik devotee, buying the Mary Janes in every colour, as well as his classic patent court shoes, which she would still describe, a decade and a half later, as 'my favourites'.

And in another dream scenario to make her former Croydon classmates jealous, 'Vivienne [Westwood] just gave me loads and loads of little things … there's this little pink and cerise mohair dress, which is really cute.'

In a photoshoot in the December issue of *i-D* magazine Kate wore a long bias-cut gold slip dress designed by Liza Bruce. Later that month, Kate would be photographed in the dress again, this time in silver, at an awards show.

The slip dress was slinky and elegant, but the sheer iridescent fabric left Kate's black briefs and bare breasts clearly visible. 'I think the body is a really beautiful thing,' Kate had said earlier that year. 'I haven't got a perfect body, but if you're comfortable with it, I think it can be.'

The silver dress somehow captured everything of Kate's style education up to that point; the crumpled 'she's come undone' glamour of Melanie's styling, the sensual confidence Mario had observed and the edgy rawness of Corinne's photography as well as Kate's own brand of mischievous showmanship.

Years later, Kate's dress, and the pants, would be displayed in a glass case at the Victoria and Albert museum.

Clearly, Kate was starting to move beyond grunge.

Kate Moss at the Los Angeles International Airport, California.

'IT HAS BEEN
WONDERFUL TO WATCH
KATE FLOURISH
OVER THE YEARS.
WHEN I FIRST MET HER
SHE WAS NO MORE
THAN A CHILD. NOW
SHE IS A TRUE
ICON OF OUR TIMES.'
Manolo Blahnik

# Story
# LA
# 4

'I got more glamorous and a bit more sophisticated ... but I wanted to dress up anyway. I liked dressing up before that, but I didn't really have anywhere to go. I didn't go to premieres then.'
KATE MOSS

Premiere of Ed Wood,
New York, 1994.

I t was Kate's clothes that brought her together with the movie star Johnny Depp. Not just the way she had dressed on the night they met; with her usual flung-together girlish confidence, in a simple satin slip and high-heeled Mary Janes, but the fact that they were still the only clothes she had with her when the snowstorm hit Manhattan early the next morning.

The night of New York's thirteenth Annual Council of Fashion Designers of America awards, 7 February 1994, must have plummeted to sub-zero temperatures. But Kate walked the red carpet alongside the parade of gala-gowned dressed-to-impress supermodels wearing a paper-thin vintage Chinese silk jacket that was only slightly shorter than the black satin slip dress underneath it, and just the sheerest of tights protecting her from the biting air.

The after-show party continued at Café Tabac, a hip bistro in the East Village. And there, at the bar,

Launch of *Kate*
autobiography,
London,
September 1995.

was Johnny Depp. 'I knew from the first moment we talked that we were going to be together,' claimed Kate. 'I went back to his hotel and we got snowed in.'

By six the following morning, the snow outside had settled in drifts, knee-deep. Kate had to call a friend to have more clothes couriered over from where she had been staying uptown. With Manhattan at a standstill, the courier took seven hours to struggle across the frozen city, through the frozen traffic. Fashion and fate had conspired to trap the pair in Depp's hotel room. 'If that hadn't happened, I don't know, we may never have phoned each other,' Kate admitted later. 'Good or bad, things are meant to be … We were together from the second we met.'

Moodily handsome, thirty-year-old Depp appeared as a throwback from other golden eras of the silver screen; shifting effortlessly from roughed up rebel-without-a-cause to slicked-back red carpet matinée idol, often in the same day. And his scruffbag-sophisticate style seemed to somehow polarise Kate's own. 'She can look twelve, and she can look like the most sophis-ticated girl you ever saw,' says designer Todd Oldham. 'You just never know what you're going to get.' At twenty, Kate could choose to dress like a woman or a girl.

By now, Kate was well used to this high–low mix of aesthetics in her life. *Times* fashion editor Lisa Armstrong recalls seeing her relaxing after the Yves Saint Laurent show in Paris, smoking in the garden at the Ritz, still in full catwalk make-up but wearing 'a droopy black sweater and skirt … skinny bare feet thrust into trainers', seemingly oblivious to her grandiose surroundings.

But Kate, the poster girl for grunge, was slowly developing a taste for luxury. Soon after meeting Depp she recalls having fallen in love with a Tiffany necklace that she had modelled on a shoot; a short, simple single strand of diamonds. 'I came home and I was like, "Oh God, this necklace I wore today…"' Depp, ever the romantic, secretly hunted it down.

Premiere of Donnie
Brasco, Century City,
February 1997.

One night, as the couple were leaving to go out to
dinner at Primrose Hill's Russian Tea Room, Depp
presented the necklace with idiosyncratic charm.
'He said, "Kate, I've got something on my arse, I
don't know what it is, but can you have a look at
it for me?" I put my hand down the back of his
trousers … and pulled out this string of Tiffany's
diamonds! Which was nice, not to find a boil!'

Kate was hooked, both on Depp ('It was really
sweet – he knows how to get the girls, for sure')
and the diamonds ('That necklace: it is a classic.
I'll never get tired of wearing that one.'). Within
four months she would respond with a thirty-first
birthday present for Johnny: a platinum 'rattle
ring', filled with tiny black pearls.

Until this point, Kate's style was almost exclusively informed by the high-octane glamour of
the 1990s fashion world, which, even during
its brief flirtation with grunge, was still charac-
terised by an in-your-face modernity that was
showy and attention-seeking, and all the things
that Kate wasn't into.

Cannes Film
Festival, 1998.

'This is from Montaldo's, a very exclusive shop,
only in a few cities in America. They'd go to
Europe and buy Dior, Balenciaga Givenchy
and Schiaparelli and then ripped the labels out!
Maybe at that time, they thought that their
name was more important.
This was one of them. Kate was always into the
little black dress. This one, with marabou
feathers, it's probably late fifties/early sixties.
The cutting is so good it gives her this hugely
hourglass figure, it gives her hips.
This would have been some of the stuff that my
brother Mark Steinberg found in the States.
He was out there travelling all over the country.
This looks like [some of] the St Louis stuff from
Mark; he went to Chicago, Dallas, Houston,
Boston, where all these socialite's wardrobes
were. And because Americans have so much
more space in their closets, they hang on to stuff.
So it's like looking for a needle in a haystack,
with bigger haystacks.
He must have seen hundreds [of dresses] in a
day and then picked out the one good one.
Most of the stuff is American, [which is] great
for her, because no one else is going to have it.
This would have been one of Mark's triumphs
- the cut is so extraordinary.'

TRACEY TOLKIEN,
STEINBERG & TOLKIEN, LONDON

CDFA awards, New York, February 1994: the night that Kate met Johnny Depp.

CDFA awards,
one year later.

But she was now becoming part of a different scene; a roll-call of beautiful people that had included Elizabeth Taylor and Richard Burton, Humphrey Bogart and Lauren Bacall, Katherine Hepburn and Spencer Tracey. The supermodels may have been the pin-ups of the day, but movie stars were icons forever.

Hollywood had a different approach to style. '[In Hollywood] it's not about wearing the clothes,' says New York vintage dealer Keni Valenti. 'Its about the woman who is wearing the clothes; the clothes don't wear you.'

Kate grasped this distinction remarkably quickly. 'She's just incredibly observant,' says fashion designer Liza Bruce. 'If you look at old photographs of actresses … the way they would just stick a jewel on; its not about wealth, its about sophistication, and she gleaned that. It's that idea of having an antique diamond bracelet, but wearing it with a T-shirt and jeans.'

And so when Kate first came to wear the Tiffany necklace, it wasn't on the red carpet (although that

65

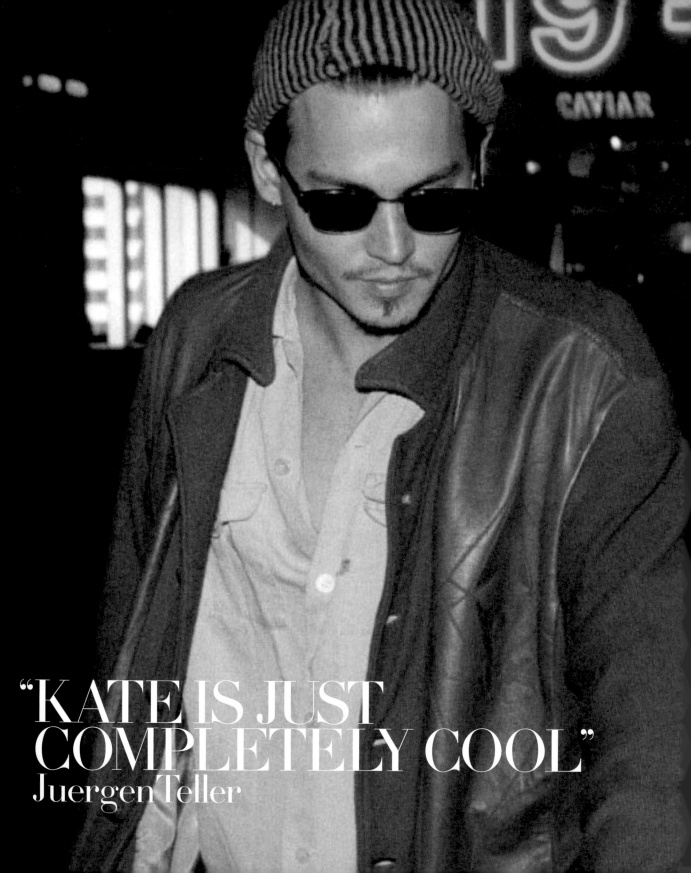

"KATE IS JUST COMPLETELY COOL"
Juergen Teller

would come); it was out on the town in London, sparkling at the neckline of a plain black T-shirt, worn with a simple satin pencil skirt, a tiny red snakeskin frame handbag and sexy, strappy snakeskin heels. Alongside Depp, in battered leather boots and jacket, the look was modern and understated, and – almost in spite of the thousand-dollar necklace – effortlessly cool.

For her red carpet wardrobe, Kate went straight to the source of Tinseltown's glamour heyday, the vintage dealers of New York and LA, who understood about fashion that lasts the test of time.

Rita Watnik, the formidable owner of Los Angeles vintage store Lie et Cie, would play a key role in Kate's Hollywood transformation. 'A lot of the first really early important vintage pieces she wore came from here,' says Watnick. By now, Kate had access to the little black books of fashion's most brilliant designers. 'Karl Lagerfeld has been coming in for, like, thirty years, and he told Kate and Naomi to come in when they were teenagers. Kate became a customer and is still a customer

now...' It would be Watnik who, years later, would present Kate with one her most iconic dresses: the frothy lemon-yellow prom dress.

Valenti was impressed with the young model's independent sense of style. 'I once said, "Kate, you have every designer at your fingertips",' he recalls. 'And she said, "I'd rather wear something that's vintage and individual, 'cos [otherwise] it's politics. And I don't want to look like everyone else."'

Kate seemingly took to Hollywood as if she'd been born to it. 'I got more glamorous and a bit more sophisticated,' says Kate of her time with Depp, 'but I wanted to dress up anyway. I liked dressing up before that, but I didn't really have anywhere to go. I didn't go to premieres then.'

Even the bare-faced girlish beauty of her teenage years was giving way to more polished touches. She told British *Vogue*, 'My most essential make-up item is my deep-red lipstick.'

She hit the red carpet for the Ed Wood premiere at September's New York film festival looking

Cannes Film Festival,
May 1997,

'I WORKED WITH KATE, STYLING HER FOR THE CERRUTI ADVERTISING CAMPAIGN. SHE FOUND THIS DRESS ON THE SHOOT, AND SHE WAS GOING TO CANNES, WITH JOHNNY. WHO WOULD HAVE THOUGHT THAT'S WHAT KATE WOULD PICK? WHO WOULD HAVE THE BALLS TO WEAR SUCH A VERY SIMPLE, VERY CHIC DRESS? BUT KATE PICKED THAT OUT. KATE DOESN'T NEED TO WEAR ANYTHING MORE THAN THAT. THAT'S KATE'S STYLE. THIS DRESS WAS A REALLY DEFINING MOMENT OF KATE'S ASCENSION INTO THAT WORLD WITH JOHNNY. AND HOW CLASSIC HER STYLE COULD BE.'

Lori Goldstein, fashion stylist, New York

every inch the starlet in a silvery beaded vintage flapper's dress believed to have been owned by Errol Flynn's wife, silent movie star Lily Damita. Kate wore the Hollywood heirloom with a light touch; her hair casually pulled back, carrying a tiny purse on a chain, with white Manolo Blahnik Mary Janes and Johnny's diamond necklace. Another time, she was spotted out on the town in a pale blue satin cheongsam dress, selling on any corner in Chinatown, and briefly caused a run on the ten-dollar dresses.

Kate and Johnny were stars. 'The first time I went to Johnny's house in LA is when I suddenly realised what I was getting myself into. I didn't realise it when we were in New York. I knew he was famous, but I didn't really know what that entailed.'

The couple seemed to lead a fairytale existence and were spotted kissing on a yacht in the Caribbean, holding hands in Aspen (with Kate in 1960s-style, furry white boots). For Christmas, Johnny gave her a Victorian diamond bracelet,

before the couple headed back to Croydon to see her family.

Perhaps Depp was the catalyst, but Kate, now in her twenties, was ready to move on from the grunge style of her teens. 'It's more fun getting dressed up in high heels and jewels and a gorgeous dress that makes you feel sexy than having to, like, work a pair of jeans and make that sexy.' A clear distinction was drawn between her personal style and her professional image, the downplayed denim street aesthetic, now shown on every corner and billboard the world over.

'She evolved rather than changed,' says Liza Bruce. 'She became more deep, more inter-esting and sophisticated.' Depp exerted a svengali influence; Kate read Jack Kerouac's 1950s Beat Generation classic *On the Road* on Depp's recommendation.

'Kate works in the fashion industry but she understands about getting influences from outside,' says Kira Joliffe. 'Johnny Depp got her on the path; he made her understand it's possible

73

With Claudia Schiffer
arriving at the Cannes
Film Festival in 1998.

'THIS IS JUST SUCH A
DEPARTURE FROM KATE'S
USUAL STYLE; THE
CLASSIC GREEK STATUE.
This is a great example of Kate
thinking, "What will other people
be wearing... what will I be
wearing... how could I stand out?",
and this is the only thing she
could have done to be different.
This is not her usual style, so that
would be pretty jaw-dropping, in a
town where everyone is dropping
each other's jaws. She was going
in the complete opposite direction
by choosing something so plain.
She looks very classical, she's not
tall, but she looks it in this.
I would have paid around £2-3000
at auction for this, for the shop.
It is very rare. Madam Gres was
the sphinx of fashion, she was a
mystery, so maybe that appealed
to Kate too. [Gres] was a wan-
nabe sculpturess, but somehow got
drawn into fashion design. She used
silk jersey, like Pucci, but solid
colours. She only ever did draping
and pleating; using it to be sculpted
to the body. Some of her things
would take 300 hours to make.
I can see why Kate would like her,
Kate fires on so many great fashion
cylinders; boho, floral prints, punk.
This is the absolute most pared
down Greek goddess style there
is. And then, wearing it to Cannes,
where it is all about that screen
goddess stuff...'

TRACEY TOLKIEN, STEINBERG
& TOLKIEN, LONDON

to have things that are irrefutably cool and stylish that the fashion industry doesn't know about.' Depp's club in LA, the Viper Room, was also a top live music venue. 'Johnny was into the Lemonheads, he understood old school rock and roll like Keith Richards, and he had an appreciation of Iggy Pop.' In his teens, Johnny's band The Kids had supported Iggy Pop on tour and the pair had co-starred in John Water's movie, *Crybaby*. 'For Kate, who was barely into her twenties, access to that kind of cultural education in the early 1990s was pretty rare. Back then, all that stuff was still pretty underground.'

Away from the red carpet, Depp continued to play his role of Hollywood maverick, singing and playing guitar in his band P and getting arrested for smashing up a hotel room. 'You have bad days,' Depp would explain later. 'Some guys go play golf; some guys smash hotel rooms.'

The pair would slouch through countless airport arrivals halls; Depp in a very Generation X knitted beanie, Kate in oddball white 1950s vintage

wayfarers, or kooky Prada trousers in a deliberately geeky print. She had a home-bleaching catastrophe with a bottle of Sun-In spray-in hair dye on the morning of a shoot for British *Vogue* and she had a tiny heart tattooed on her hand. He revised his inked tribute to ex-fiancée Winona Ryder from 'Winona Forever' to 'Wino Forever'.

Like any rebel without a cause, Depp's dress sense was artfully careless. 'Johnny has worn the same boots every day for twenty years,' says James Brown. 'I used to try to hide them so he couldn't find them.'

This anarchic approach to fashion extended towards Kate's clothes too. Depp threw a surprise party for her twenty-first birthday. 'Johnny said, "We're going to dinner – put a dress on," and I'm like, "I haven't got a dress." So I had on this satin dress, down to the floor, and he got the scissors and he's, like, cutting it up to the knee, literally, while we're walking out the door. I'm wearing, like, red satin up to the knee, all jagged.'

Depp took her to the Viper Room, where her

'I CANNOT THINK OF A BETTER TESTAMENT TO KATE'S CHIC, GLAMOUR AND BEAUTY THAN THE PROOF OF HER ABILITY TO TURN A SIMPLE SLIP-UNADORNED, NOR OVERLY-ACCESSORIZED-INTO A GOWN FIT FOR A GODDESS!' Marc Jacobs

In Marc Jacobs, 1996.

friends and family from all over the world were waiting. Disco legends Thelma Houston and Gloria Gaynor sang her Happy Birthday. Depp lavished her with presents including a quirky first edition of *Alice in Wonderland* with illustrations by Salvador Dali.

John Galliano gave her an exquisitely simple white bias-cut slip dress, which would become one of her all-time favourites. She wore it – along with the diamond bracelet Depp gave her for Christmas and the Tiffany necklace – to the CFDA (Council of Fashion Designers of America) fashion awards on the couple's one-year anniversary. Kate's twelve-month transformation from girlish low-key cool to polished sophisticate was remarkable.

Depp would often act with old-fashioned panache. When Kate admired a dress film star Julie Christie wore in the political comedy *Shampoo*, Depp secretly had an identical dress custom-made for Kate as a surprise. A glossy, black sequinned floor-length gown, with long sleeves and a high neck, the seemingly demure dress was actually backless. Kate wore the show-stopping gown to the 1995 Golden Globes, and again to the CFDA awards in 1998.

Kate didn't have an official stylist, but she did have help. Her long-term friend James Brown, now also living in New York, was starting to progress beyond merely styling Kate's hair.

In 1995 fashion designer Sue Stemp moved into James's West Village apartment, with Kate living just around the corner on Waverly Place. Ever since Sue met James in a Brixton club wearing a Vivienne Westwood deerstalker hat, he has, she says, 'always had a really good look of his own going on, but James's sense of fashion and style goes way beyond his own personal look, and his work'.

In New York, James was in his element. 'He can't physically walk past a second-hand shop without going in and finding something within seconds that would "look great on Kate". It's such a talent. He not only can find something out of nothing that will really work on Kate, but he visualises the whole look on her; from the hair to her tights to her shoes. A girl's best friend.'

In 1995 Kate published a biography, a photography book called, simply, *Kate*. For the launch party she wore a belted figure-hugging vintage black dress with a strappy neckline, delicate high heels and deep red nails; pure polished 1950s movie-star style. Kate was learning the simple statement power of the little black dress, which she would repeat for many years to come (so much so that this dress, and a strapless feather trim dress,

would be worn again and again over the years).

'Kate was always into the little black dress,' recalls Tracey Tolkein, claiming that over the years 'she had bought maybe 60 to 75 little black dresses ranging from late 1940s to the late 1960s'.

Kate's cocktail dresses were the perfect style statement for a woman who was swiftly becoming a fixture in the Hollywood establishment. In November 1995, she wore the strapless feather-trim dress to a live performance by Frank Sinatra at the Shrine Auditorium in Los Angeles. '[Sinatra] came up and started flirting with me,' she says. 'I went to put my hand out and he kissed me on the lips.' That same night, she met Bob Dylan 'and I nearly fainted'.

As Kate's confidence had grown on the red carpet, and as her fame grew, her look became increasingly pared down. The 1997 Cannes Film Festival presented an iconic image of Kate, wearing a simple pale grey shift dress among all the glitz. 'This was really the defining moment of Kate's ascension into that world with Johnny,' says Lori Goldstein, who styled the Cerutti advertising campaign photoshoot on which Kate had discovered the dress.

The grey dress was a seminal example of what would become one of Kate's distinctive style quirks, 'going the other way' and subtly rebelling against the expected dress code. According to Goldstein, the quietly elegant dress betrayed an unshakeable confidence. 'That's Kate's style; she doesn't need to wear anything more than that,' says Goldstein. The dress catapulted her onto Best Dressed lists worldwide.

The couple, both at the top of their respective careers, were increasingly in demand, and often out of town or overseas in different countries and different time-zones. Kate found herself frequently alone and listless in LA, 'And Johnny says, "Well, go shopping then".' Unable to drive, Kate would head off in the back of a chauffeur-driven car, scouring the vintage stores in Los Angeles. 'He was away a lot of the time, and I'd go shopping, do that ladies-who-lunch crap, faff around. It was so boring – the most lonely shallow place. I was going insane. I'm not normally a depressed person, but I brooded, got really sad – and we grew apart.'

The couple made their last appearance together at Cannes in 1998, with Kate statuesque in a simple white column vintage dress by couturier Madame Gres.

In her early twenties, Kate's taste had started to take another unexpected turn.

London, 2006.

# 'KATE WAS ALWAYS INTO THE LITTLE BLACK DRESS

## Tracey Tolkein

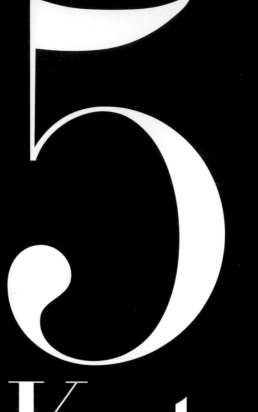

# 5

'Clothes go in and out of fashion, but that's not real style. Style has to be classic.'
**KATE MOSS**

# Kate.
# Britannia

At a private
party in London,
June 1994.

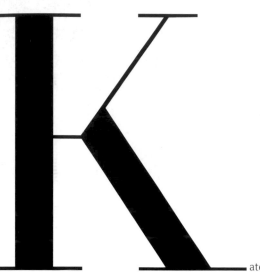

K

In a Clements
Ribeiro Union Jack
jumper, 1997.

ate had bought herself a $3,000 Hermes Birkin bag for her twenty-first birthday in sky blue denim and tan leather. 'It was so gorgeous! I just thought it was the most perfect bag!' For Kate, it was. The bag was originally designed in 1984 for singer and actress Jane Birkin, an effortlessly stylish woman with a nonchalant attitude to fashion and luxury. A decade later, Birkin would doubtless have approved of Kate's choice; a younger, more irreverent twist on the deluxe bag.

'Kate with her little Birkin!' Lori Goldstein remembers. 'Of course, the Birkin is awesome, and now they're everywhere. But to know that bag was amazing back then ... she was obsessed way before anyone else.'

Kate wasn't one for status symbols, or logos, but she did appreciate quality. The girl who – diamonds aside – still preferred thrift stores to designer boutiques had been prompted to make some big tag purchases by an eye-opening meeting with her accountant, who that year had sat her down and finally revealed her personal fortune. Kate went straight out with Sarah Doukas and bought an £800 Vivienne Westwood sheepskin coat to celebrate, later describing it as her proudest purchase.

At this time, Kate's wardrobe was all over the place. Not her style, of course, but her now vast collection of clothes. Constantly travelling worldwide, but mainly living in the States with Johnny and without a permanent UK base of her own (she'd bought a flat in Shepherd's Bush, but had never moved in, staying instead in her previous lodgings with photographer Marc Lebon), the bulk of Kate's clothes were stored in boxes, piled up in the downstairs loo of the London flat belonging to her long-suffering assistant Jess.

In 1994 Kate met Fran Cutler 'at the Atlantic bar – Kate was sitting there with her mum. I knew she was good friends with John Galliano, because [DJ] Jeremy Healy, who I was representing, used to do the music for John's shows. Through me, she started hanging out with Meg and Noel [Gallagher, of Oasis]. So we had all these connections through fashion and music.'

The mid-1990s were the height of Britpop. Oasis and Blur were referencing the music of the 1960s; The Beatles and The Kinks. Meg and Noel's house, Supernova Heights, located a few doors down from The Beatles' famous recording studios on Abbey Road, was the epicentre of the scene.

Here, the two generations of rock royalty collided. 'Kate's more of a Stones fan than anything else,' says Cutler, 'and we all hung out with Marlon ...' Kate was already friends with Keith Richards and Anita Pallenberg's son Marlon, who was married to YSL model Lucie de la Falaise. Marlon introduced Kate and Johnny to Keith, Ronnie Wood and the rest of the Stones, and through them, she met Anita Pallenberg and Marianne Faithfull (Mick Jagger's ex).

'The more Kate has got to travel the world, the more she's got to meet her idols,' says Lori Goldstein. 'Keith and Marianne are the coolest people of that generation, and Kate just fits right in. She's classic rock 'n' roll.'

And so was Johnny Depp, an accomplished guitarist who Noel Gallagher invited to play slide guitar on his single 'Fade Away'. When Noel chose to re-record the song for a War Child charity record, Kate and Johnny flew over. Kate played tambourine and hung out with the other

'That jumper was actually modelled by Naomi Campbell originally, a key look of our "Punk Trousseau" collection for A/W 97. 97/98 was all about "cool Britannia" and that sweater became emblematic of that time because it so happily summarised that moment: the eccentric polish of the feathers and the Manolos, the Union Jack in Scottish cashmere, the layback glamour down to the tattooed tights – all you miss is Oasis in the background and that moment is totally captured. Kate rushed to our showroom in Paris [at the hyper cool, freshly opened Hotel Costes] immediately after the show and introduced herself. She was completely into the collection and started trying everything on as the buyers looked on, stunned. In the end she ordered twenty-two pieces (and boosted our sales in the process as the buyers quickly adjusted their orders to reflect her selection.) When we delivered them to her two months later she sent us a huge bouquet of flowers with a charming thank you note – something no other model or celebrity has ever done before and since, in our experience! For weeks afterwards, a day wouldn't go past without a "Kate sighting" in one our pieces. The following season she opened and closed our show.
The fact that she liked and enjoyed those pieces so much is most flattering because Kate has a real passion for clothes.
Yes, I'm sure she loves her job and possibly even cares about fashion, but her thrill and her passion are in the actual frocks. Her style is not a random accident of timing and opportunism; it is is born of a very specific taste, a very discerning and confident eye as well as a fabulous knack for throwing things.'

INACIO RIBEIRO, CLEMENTS RIBEIRO, LONDON

musicians, including Paul and Linda McCartney, and their daughter Stella, then studying fashion design at Central St Martins.

So even while she was still living in America with Johnny, Kate kept in touch with her British roots. When Pulp's Jarvis Cocker ambushed Michael Jackson's egocentric performance at the 1996 Brit Awards, Kate asked a stylist friend to make up 'Jarvis is Jesus' T-shirts, and she and Naomi wore them backstage at the Milan shows.

Later that summer, she flew back to the UK for Oasis's landmark Knebworth concert, and introduced her mum to the McCartneys. 'Mum was like, "I'm not washing ever again".'

*Newsweek* was suddenly calling London 'the coolest city on the planet'. *Vanity Fair*'s March 1997 cover announced 'London swings again', and Kate appeared, wrapped in the national flag, a Clements Ribeiro cashmere Union Flag jumper, to launch London Fashion Week, declaring, 'London's booming again, I love to be in London.'

Within the year her relationship with Johnny had ended, and she returned to London permanently. 'She lived with Meg and Noel for a bit when she came back from America,' says Fran. So Kate was now in residence at Supernova Heights, party central, and the Buckingham Palace of Cool Britannia.

'There were suddenly all these amazing British designers and then she was there in the centre of it all, already a supermodel,' says fashion designer Matthew Williamson, who was among the new generation of British design talent.

Kate's patronage had become an invaluable commodity, capable of launching a new label into the big league overnight. Mick Jagger's daughter Jade, who discovered Williamson when she had worn one of his earliest pieces in a Tatler photoshoot, offered to model if Matthew put on a show and brought Kate round to the designer's tiny bedsit on Grays Inn Road. 'Kate was in her heyday, and we sat on the floor eating McDonalds; all very non-glamorous. She said "Right, I'll do it [the show]. But I want to wear this," and pulled out the pink cowl dress and blue dragonfly cardigan.' The day after the show Kate and Jade were on the front page of every paper.

'I realised the importance and impact for an unknown designer of having Kate involved,' says Williamson. 'I owe a lot to her; I felt very flattered. She could pick and choose at that point what she wanted to do.'

Kate also supported Stella McCartney, and had modelled alongside Naomi Campbell in her St Martins graduate fashion show. Stella had trained in Savile Row, and her sexy take on the traditional trouser suit, paired with candy-coloured silk blouses and camisoles, soon took the fashion world by storm.

At this time, another Savile Row-trained designer was making his mark on the London fashion scene. Alexander McQueen's tailoring was more sharply cut and aggressive in detailing with slashed and bloodied motifs. McQueen's iconoclastic designs were, however, hugely influential (his infamous buttock-revealing bumster trousers caused outrage and ridicule, but kick-started a decade of low-cut hipster trouser styles).

Fellow mavericks in the rarefied world of fashion, McQueen and Kate were drawn to each other. 'Kate Moss is his kind of woman,' says designer Julien Macdonald. 'He would always think, "Would Kate like that?" [about his designs] They've got a mutual understanding for each other.'

Both McQueen and McCartney were pushing traditional tailoring with a twist. And alongside New York designer Marc Jacobs' deluxe basics, classic was starting to look cool again.

Kate was now hanging out with an older crowd. 'Back in the day it was pretty much Kate and Marianne [Faithfull], and me and Anita [Pallenberg],' recalls artist and fashion designer Dan Macmillan. Kate's approach to dressing seemed to mature too: 'I can dress my mum in my clothes and it doesn't look wrong; I can go shopping with Marianne and we can try on the same dress. I don't know why, but people are just wearing the same things.'

Sometimes literally, there was a communality and clothes swapping among her new friends. Anita passed on her original Biba playsuit, realising Kate would appreciate it. Kira Joliffe noted '[they understand that fashion] It's not a consumer thing; it's just about being into clothes. Really liking good clothes and it really, really, really doesn't matter where things come from.'

It was about 'willingly sharing style by passing it around,' she continued. 'It's not about stealing each other's style; it's about a cool blurring of ideas. I've been on the receiving end of Anita's generosity. Anita Pallenberg is very generous … she's not selling [her] stuff on eBay.'

*Pop* magazine editor and stylist Katie Grand first worked with Kate on a shoot for *Dazed and Confused* in October 1997. 'We were previewing Stella McCartney's first collection for Chloe – they hadn't even had the show yet – and [photographer] Juergen [Teller] had Kate rolling around in the back yard in these precious silk dresses.' At that time,

the stylist was struck that 'Kate always had pretty simple clothes, but amazing taste in jewellery.'

'She's always been fascinated with jewellery,' says Versace stylist Brana Wolf. 'We were like kids around Donatella [Versace]'s jewels. Donatella would wear jewellery and we'd be like, "That's amaaaaazing." There would be an "Ooh!" The famous Kate Moss "Ooh!"'

'I do specifically remember a jewellery period,' says Wolf. 'That's another side of Kate's really great eye; nothing screams [for attention]. She will just be wearing some fabulous bracelet; you're not going to see Kate with tons of things around her neck.'

Wolf recalls bumping into Kate and Naomi in Italy. 'I remember having lunch with the two of them and they'd been on a jewellery shopping spree in Milan. They brought out these little sacks ...' Kate had treated herself to a pair of nineteenth-century Spanish emerald earrings in 18-carat gold.

Once again, Kate was able to get great recommendations, claiming the jewellery store Pennisi was 'the same place Miuccia [Prada] buys hers, so they must be all right'. But Wolf claims it was Campbell who was encouraging Kate's extravagant spending. 'I think it might have been Naomi who went there [first].'

Liza Bruce also remembers Kate's jewellery period. 'She told me she decided, "I'm going to put my money in antique jewellery", instead of splashing out on, I guess, modern clothes. That's really shrewd. You might want something, like a fab coat. But no, she's going to invest in antique jewellery, from places like SJ Philips [in Old Bond Street]. Proper jewellery.'

Other than diamonds, Kate's greatest extravagance was Manolo Blahnik shoes; by now, she owned over 100 pairs, ranging from the classic stiletto-heeled patent court shoes to chunky strappy snakeskin sandals, delicate ankle-tie zebra-print evening shoes or her trademark girly Mary Janes. But Kate wore them as casually as she had her Adidas trainers; the patent court shoes were worn with black ankle socks and turned-up Levi's jeans.

Kate's low-key approach to luxury wasn't without high-fashion elements. She kept the much-coveted blue velvet hipsters that she had modelled in Tom Ford's blockbuster first show for Gucci, but wore them with a skinny vintage leather jacket and a simple $25 thrift store navy cashmere polo neck (rather than the disco-sexy electric blue stretchy silk shirt from the catwalk); fitting in with her favourite fashion mantra, from which

Halloween party at the Supper Club in New York, 1997.

she has never swerved: 'Never wear anything, designer or high-street, head-to-toe.'

Despite now being the poster girl for street-style denim worldwide, with her rolling CK Jeans contract, Kate's favourite Calvin Klein piece was in fact a camel crombie; a classically tailored overcoat, neatly cut for even a petite model like Kate to look chic, worn with simple pieces; a white vest, a black A-line skirt, with grey Prada Mary Janes and leopard-print bag. Over time the crombie had acquired, as *Vogue* noted, a 'suitable secondhand patina'.

Worn-in was Kate's favourite look. Asked to comment on a selection of high-street clothes for *Vogue*, Kate zeroed in on a pair of Ravel sandals in a faded snakeskin print saying approvingly, 'What's good about these is that they look slightly old as if they were a second-hand find.'

In her early twenties, when most girls would still be chasing cheap copycat versions of catwalk looks in high-street stores, Kate was already beyond that. '[I don't] wear high-street – I either buy designer or second-hand; I either go to thrift shops and buy something for 10p, or I'll spend money and buy a really good cashmere jumper.'

'She wears smart stuff,' vintage dealer Tracey Tolkien says simply.

'She just has damn good taste,' says Wolf. 'I think that she does have an innate [dress] sense really on the classic side, but always the coolest most updated classic. So what she chooses is absolutely the most current version of that. Women have been dressing like that for years, but she takes it to a very contemporary level; a jean, a great shoe, a beautiful jacket. But her jean will be super-skinny; the jacket will be shrunken.'

Even with her seemingly timeless choices, Kate warns, 'Above all … don't expect anything to last for ever.' Kate wore her classics with a youthful carelessness. 'To further make it contemporary and desirable, her hair looks natural. There's an absence of a lot of make-up,' says Wolf, 'so she embodies this very desirable look that is sexy and chic at that same time … and she does it all on her small frame.' Kate is tiny; a UK size 6 (US size 4).

'She was smaller than the rest of the models; but I don't just mean skinny,' says Tracey Tolkien. 'She has bought lots of Ossie Clark and it suits her because of the proportions; he was dressing people raised in wartime during rationing, so they were tiny. On the taller models [Ossie's designs] didn't work so well.'

'I love Ossie Clark,' said Kate. 'His clothes fit me like a dream.' Kate had been a fan of the designer since her Portobello Market days, but she was now hanging out with Ossie's original clients, Marianne Faithfull and even Mick Jagger and The Beatles, who Clark created stage-wear for in the late 1960s. Kate also had an appreciation for the legacy of the label.

'She was one of the first people to start buying Ossie Clark again,' says Tolkien. 'She recognised it was fantastic, beautiful cutting. She bought tons.'

Kate was already very particular when it came to the cut of her clothes. By now she had attended endless pre-catwalk show fittings, where garments are expertly and precisely tailored to each model's body. Kate favoured a cut that 'really, you know, fits under the arms'. Vintage dealer Jeff Ihenacho regularly had pieces altered for Kate's petite frame. 'She always wants things to fit in the torso; that's really important to her,' he says.

Kate's understanding of the importance of fit played a key role in the confident appearance of her many looks. Her trademark tight-to-the-torso silhouette was a simple but subtly effective device in contributing to her ability to always look as if clothes were made for her, as if no one else but Kate could ever have worn them.

'The most stylish women I know have a formula,' says Matthew Willamson, 'so despite the fact they move with the times and they adapt to trends accordingly, the bigger umbrella of what does or doesn't suit them remains. Kate could wear any era of clothing and she would come out looking amazing.'

Off the catwalk, Kate rarely wore bright colours, but for the odd piece of knitwear: a fuchsia Clements Ribeiro V-neck cashmere jumper; a red Vivienne Westwood skinny-knit cardigan. 'You don't often see her in a lot of colour,' says Matthew Williamson. 'When I think of her style I certainly don't think of bright colours. Every woman has insecurities about their body or skin tone so I'm sure she has similar criteria when getting ready; maybe garish colour doesn't work for her. She wears more monochrome, chic gentle colours, fleshy tones or greys and blacks. You dress according to your environment, the colours of the place you live. And we're quite a grey nation.'

'But she'll play with print in a very timeless way,' says Williamson. 'Anita [Pallenberg] has that timelessness too; playing with print like its never going to date; it's not [just] the print of the moment.'

Sure enough, at that time, Kate was obsessed with 1960s psychedelic print designer Emilio Pucci. 'I remember her buying a lot of Pucci from us,' says Katy Rodriguez, owner of Resurrection vintage in New York. 'We'd just try to find her loads and loads of Pucci and kept it for her.' Kate's first purchase

from the store was a rich blue Pucci print coat.

The increasing spotlight on her personal wardrobe, as well as having recently published her autobiography, was making Kate think about her style legacy. When *Vogue* asked to photograph Kate 'in her own style' she was uncompromising. 'None of them are things I want to be photographed in, or remembered as my style,' she said, rejecting even her simple Stella McCartney navy slip dress. 'Clothes go in and out of fashion, but that's not real style. Style has to be classic.' She was finally photographed naked in her antique emerald earrings – very Kate.

'Kate seems to be very confident in her taste,' says Katie Grand. 'The only other person who I know who is so secure is Miuccia Prada.'

For evening, Kate's key piece was the statement coat; from a black and white pony spotted vintage coat, to a pale blue cashmere coat with a fur collar, the Calvin Klein crombie, the Galliano Union Flag jacket, and a sumptuously ruched blue velvet evening coat.

Her favourite party outfit was still the dress John Galliano gave her for her twenty-first birthday: 'My best ever good time party dress,' said Kate. 'I still wear it and I always have a good time in it. If I was going to wear it tonight I would put it with a pair of silver strappy shoes and my blue [velvet] coat.'

Kate has 'lots of dresses with trains' but, she laments, 'nobody dresses up anymore – which is a shame. I just think it's really nice to dress for dinner and dress for … well, y'know, dress for occasions.'

Kate's life was becoming increasingly like the F. Scott Fitzgerald novels she loved to read. Hungover one summer morning and desperate to get out of the city, in a 'moment of clarity' Kate called her film director friend David Rocksavage, the seventh Marquess of Cholmondeley, to suggest escaping to his Norfolk country house, Houghton Hall.

Slipping on a Galliano gown, and throwing little more than cigarettes and a tiara in her bag, Kate jumped barefoot into a car to Battersea helipad. After landing in the grounds of the eighteenth-century Palladian stately home, they sipped champagne and smoked cigarettes on the vast lawns. As the sun set and the moon rose, surrounded by peacocks and white deer, with her host playing the piano somewhere in the near distance, Kate had a moment of déjà vu: 'Suddenly I thought, "Oh my god! I am in *The Great Gatsby*."'

Kate had a dressing-up chest at her new home in

London, 1997.

the smart St Johns Wood area of North London. 'I love to create this fantasy kind of thing,' she says. 'Dressing is fun. Otherwise things are boring. Dressing makes everything fun. It makes clothes fun, it makes getting up fun and it makes going to bed more interesting.'

For a model, dressing up is all in a day's work. The catwalk shows, following John Galliano's lead, were becoming increasingly theatrical. Even younger designers like Alexander McQueen created spectacles with animal heads, paint-spraying robots and rain on the catwalk. ('It was great, a great show, walking through that water!' said an exhilarated Kate, backstage.)

Kate dressed up as a cowboy in tiny denim hot pants and a Stetson hat for Ronnie Wood's Wild West themed fiftieth birthday. Surrounded by the greatest hedonists of a generation, it was Kate who was the life and soul of the party.

'You always feel she enjoys the process of dressing,' says Wolf. 'I remember one Halloween party she gave in New York; she loved having everyone dress up.' Kate had arrived with a top hat and cane, wearing a gothic black lace gown, her knickers and suspender belt visible underneath.

Kate's new party partner in crime was Donatella Versace. 'They are both fun party people,' says Brana. 'Kate's got that adorable laugh, and Donatella is just fun and funny and dry.'

Vogue party, 1998.

'She came in one day together with Anita Pallenberg and they were looking for something for a shoot they were doing. I don't remember which magazine it was, no. It was in 1995 or 1996 I think. They both tried on so many things that day, and Kate took this coat. Everything in Voyage was a one-off. It was all unique — nothing was made twice; we would change the colour, or the fabric, or something. And she chose this velvet coat in royal blue. It has a padded collar, and the colour is vibrant because it was over-dyed — dyed as a finished piece — as all our pieces were. It was quite an eccentric piece, and I think she fell for that.'

LOUISE MAZZILLI,
VOYAGE, LONDON

Heathrow
Airport, 1997

With Meg
Matthews,
London, 1997.

Leaving San
Lorenzo's
after a meal
with her mother

With Marianne
Faithfull at
the Costume
Insitute Gala,
New York, 1997.

The Rock for Dockers
evening at the Sound
Republic, London, 1998.

Director John Bland remembers, 'We were all at a party in New York, at Donatella's house uptown, and Kate was telling me to nick Donatella's shoes [while] she was asleep on the couch. She wanted them because they had diamond butterflies on, before the butterflies were big. Kate's a proper party girl. She knows how to have fun.'

Kate's friendship with Donatella deepened after her brother Gianni Versace's shocking murder in 1997. 'When Kate was with all the [supermodels] and then Gianni died they were the girls who were really close to Donatella,' says Lori Goldstein 'and she really felt protected by them. That group of girls really cared about Donatella and they really rallied around.'

Kate attended Gianni's memorial with Marianne, who wrote in her memoirs, 'I went with Kate Moss, who was wearing a beautiful old Versace number she owned.' An off-the-shoulder knee-length little black dress, it was stretchy but demure.

Kate's growing collection of Versace dresses, mostly presents from Donatella, were more redolent of Kate's classic taste than Versace's va-va-voom sexiness, like the simple strapless grey wool dress, tailored neatly to her petite body, that she wore to a London film premiere with Meg Mathews.

One of Kate's last appearances that year was on the Versace catwalk, her hair dyed bright pink. The partying was starting to spiral out of control. 'It was just a build-up, really. I was definitely living fast … I was not very happy. I was doing things that weren't good for me,' says Kate. 'I got tired of feeling like Dracula. I wanted to see some daylight and not just at six o'clock in the morning.'

In November Kate checked into the Churchill Priory clinic for four weeks' rehab treatment.

Kate entered the Priory a party animal (she checked in wearing dark glasses) and came out a born-again hippy. She disappeared on holiday with Marianne to Marrakech (favoured retreat of The Beatles and The Rolling Stones thirty years earlier).

In January, following an appearance on the Versace catwalk, Donatella threw Kate a twenty-fifth birthday party in a Paris nightclub, presenting her with a set of ruby, sapphire and diamond bracelets. 'Kate was really touched,' remembers Lori Goldstein, who had styled Kate's first modelling job since leaving rehab: a Versace jeans advertising campaign with Stephen Meisel. 'These relationships are way more than fashion; [it's] true friendship.'

Kate had taken up yoga, had her house

'This was a pink top made of devoré which we sold. It was very very tight – almost like a second skin, or something that has been tattooed on the body. It was very sexy. But then Kate is very sexy anyway. This was over-dyed, so that the pieces took on a special quality. And I think Kate liked that – I don't believe someone like Kate wants to be with people who are wearing the same things as her. I love her for that!'
LOUISE MAZZILLI, VOYAGE, LONDON

exorcised, and was reading *The Tao of Pooh* [bear]. She now had a dog, (named Sid after Sid Vicious), and was even trying horse riding. She saw a counsellor once a week, and attended Alcoholics Anonymous and Narcotics Anonymous meetings as often as possible. She bought a house in the country, which was being feng shui'd.

Her look was changing too. She described a favourite outfit: 'blonde pashmina, Stella McCartney trousers frayed round the hems; vintage rabbit top thing; Lainey Keogh gold cummerbund; embroidered Chinese slippers; old Brian Jones coat by Ossie Clark'.

Matthew Williamson, whose own colourfully embellished designs were inspired by his trips to rich hippy hotspots Ibiza and India, suggests that influence may have come from Pallenberg: 'Anita is definitely at the hippy end of the spectrum; she's much more of an eclectic dresser than a minimalist.'

Kate's latest jewellery purchase was a huge natural pearl ring; the perfect choice for a jet-set hippy, and she was buying pretty embellished pieces: sparkly hair clips and embroidered skirts from boho boutique The Cross, and cute ribbon trimmed tops at the exclusive rich hippy store Voyage on the Kings Road.

Kate had a new lifestyle and a new look. But neither would last for long.

# 6 Changes

'I'd been saying for years, 'Shall I cut my hair?
Shall I cut my hair? Shall I cut my hair?'
And my friend was like, 'Kate, for God's sake,
shut up! Just cut it.' So I did that day.
I was looking at pictures of Edie Sedgwick.'
KATE MOSS

Kate and Liv Tyler
at the Chloe fashion
show, Paris, 2001.

**Y**ears later Kate would claim there had never been a point when she realised that women were trying to dress like her. But the earliest example of Kate's personal style causing a fashion storm was the moment in January 2000 when she wore a vintage pair of battered, buckled, slouchy Vivienne Westwood boots from the designer's 1981 Pirate collection to a Santana concert in London.

'If people had told me a girl could create a stir like this over a pair of bloody boots, I would never have believed them,' says Steven Phillips, who had found the boots for Kate.

That year, Steven had upgraded from a Portobello Market stall to open Rellik, an upmarket vintage clothing store at the foot of the iconic Trellick Tower, a stone's throw from the market. A long-time collector, he already had a love of Vivienne Westwood clothes in common with Kate.

From the moment they met, Steven played a key role in Kate's style, regularly handpicking pieces for her and eventually becoming so prolific in his assistance that he would often send over a bag of clothes a week for her to consider.

Clearly Kate had a great deal of help with

Kate and Fran Cutler
London, 2000.

Carlos Santana's gig at
the Tabernacle, Notting
hill, London, 2000.

Kate and
Jade Jagger,
London, 1999.

British Designer
of the Year
Awards, 1999.

With Tom Ford at David Bailey's 60th birthday party and book launch, Claridges, London, 2001.

sourcing clothes; more than the average customer. But ultimately the choice of what to wear was hers alone.

Kira Joliffe remembers bumping into Kate at a party she was hosting for her magazine *Cheap Date*. Kate was wearing the pirate boots: 'I had two pairs, and [I told her] the cobbler who made them was closing. Kate knew about the guy who made them [because] Bella Freud was really into them because she had worked at Vivienne Westwood.

'I was telling her all this and you could see she was taking in what was being said about these shoes. It wasn't just that someone had given her these boots and said that they were cool; she was engaged with the history and the background of these boots.'

'With Kate, the elements are not really important,' says Marc Jacobs. 'It's the sum of them that's important.' The boots were part of a new look that Kate was now adopting, a kind of nonchalant London girl look; a pseudo-skint scruffiness that belied her status as a multi-millionairess, but seemed to fit perfectly with her gig-going, chain-smoking and unapologetically louche return to the party circuit.

Kate had worn the pirate boots with bare

legs and a tiny denim miniskirt enveloped in a gigantic khaki parka. A month later, Kate wore the parka again; with a vintage Westwood miniskirt, an orange Courreges jumper and 1950s mesh heels that she had bought that afternoon from One of a Kind vintage on Portobello Road. 'She was just going out to Fulham – Jesse [Wood] was performing,' says owner Jeff Ihenacho, referring to Ronnie Wood's son, who Kate was briefly dating.

London was soon wall-to-wall with girls in miniskirts and heels worn with outsized parkas. *Pop* editor Katie Grand recalls, 'I was sharing a flat with Luella (Bartley) at the time and we both shared parkas, and in the first issue of *Pop* we wrote about the popularity of parkas.'

Kate made being scruffy seem like a style statement, barefaced but for her signature teenager-style make-up, 'black eyeliner, always' and scraped-back hair. 'I don't really think Kate is that bothered about what people think of her,' says Grand.

Yet Kate was incredibly influential, even among her friends. The day after Kate came in to One of a Kind, Meg Mathews, Fran Cutler and Davinia Taylor appeared. 'She came in and they all came.

Celebrating Matthew
Williamson's Fall/Winter
2001 Collection, New
York, June 2001.

'THIS SKIRT WAS MADE OUT OF FRENCH LACE AND BEADED IN LITTLE FACETED CRYSTALS. IT WAS ALSO WORN BY SARAH JESSICA PARKER IN SEX AND THE CITY AND WAS VERY POPULAR AT THE TIME. IT WAS A REALLY SPECIAL PIECE, QUITE PRECIOUS, AND IT HAD AN ANTIQUE QUALITY TO IT, SO IT WAS VINTAGE YET QUITE FOXY AND SHORT. KATE WORE IT TO A PARTY OF MINE AT BUNGALOW 8 IN NEW YORK. SHE CAME WITH JUDE AND SADIE.'

Matthew Williamson,
designer, London

With
Jefferson
Hack.

There are just some people we look up to – she has some incredible style,' says Ihenacho.

Rellik was suddenly receiving 200 calls a month about the boots. 'She was photographed in them, and suddenly everyone wanted a pair,' says Steven. 'It was all because of Kate.'

Vintage Westwood pirate boots were now selling for a fortune on eBay, high-street stores started making their own versions, and within the year Westwood herself put the original boots back into production; Kate was now influencing her own fashion idols. But for a style rebel mainly concerned with having an original look, Kate had mixed feelings about the sudden epidemic of pirate boots: 'Oh no, that means I can't wear them anymore.'

But her look was about to take a more radical change in direction. Kate cut her hair. Bored, during a spell in hospital 'for a kidney infection', James Brown cut off her signature long tousled hair into a sleek gamine crop, shaved at the back, with a long sweeping fringe.

'I'd been saying for years, "Shall I cut my hair? Shall I cut my hair? Shall I cut my hair?"' says Kate. 'And my friend was like, "Kate, for God's sake, shut up! Just cut it." So I did that day. I was

'She found a very demure, beautiful Audrey Hepburn-style black cocktail dress, with tiny sleeves, black satin, and gathered at the waist. It was another dress by Montaldo's which was actually a department store in America in the Forties and Fifties. They'd have things by Schiaparelli and Chanel and they would take their labels out, they wanted it to be their label in it. So anything from Montaldo's is very hard to find; most of the stuff is American, and great for Kate, because no one else is going to have it - even with a piece by Biba or Ossie Clark other people would show up in it. And she wore it to the British Fashion Awards.'

TRACEY TOLKIEN,
STEINBERG &
TOLKIEN VINTAGE,
LONDON

British Fashion
Awards, 2001.

'I think it was a shift dress,
I don't think it has sleeves.
It just has that beautiful lace
on the neckline. Kate came in
with (model) Frankie Rayder,
and was showing her around.
Frankie hadn't been in before,
but Kate had bought loads
of stuff from me... And the
two of them bought tons of
stuff. They were both really
like excited about Cannes.
And then after, Kate called
me and said "look on the
internet" and she showed
me this photo of the two
of them at Cannes, both
wearing dresses that they'd
got from me. And they
both looked gorgeous...'
KENI VALENTI, KENI
VALENTI VINTAGE, NEW YORK

looking at pictures of Edie Sedgwick.'

It was Kate's most extreme transformation to date. 'Kate's a chameleon,' says Tom Ford. 'Madonna is a chameleon as well, which ultimately means they are timeless.'

Ford subsequently named Kate as his muse. '[She] was definitely an inspiration for me this season. Kate was the perfect embodiment for the spring [2001] collection.' Kate appeared on the Gucci catwalk in a fitted corset dress and white ankle boots, with her newly peroxided sleek blonde bob. 'Like a good fashion designer, Kate anticipates what people want,' says Ford. 'Whether it is cerebral or intuitive, she manages to pull from the air the spirit of the moment and embody it.'

'The short blonde hair was amazing for her career,' says James. 'But that was the last thing we were thinking. She was going to give up modelling!'

Kate wanted to quit. She called the agency and told them she'd had enough. 'I quit because I thought, "I ... hate it".'

Doukas was sympathetic. 'If you've had a career that long, with no breaks, you're bound to get fed up, and she was.' Kate was eventually dissuaded from turning her back on the industry.

After rehab, Kate had seemed less comfortable being in the public eye. In an interview with photographer friend Juergen Teller, she claimed fame 'has taken away a lot, my privacy for example'. Asked how she copes with such relentless attention, she said simply, 'I go away a lot.'

Although this too had its disadvantages; while away in the media spotlight at the New York shows in October 2000, thieves broke into her St Johns Wood house, taking thousands of pounds worth of jewellery, including the diamond necklace from Johnny.

On the red carpet with Liv Tyler at a London film premiere in April 2001, Kate teasingly rebuffed the waiting reporters with the statement, 'No, I don't speak.' A casual joke, with some truth to it. This mystique was starting to capture the world's imagination. In an era of fame-hungry reality show stars (Big Brother had begun the previous summer) and celebrity magazines (Heat was only in its third year), Kate seemed more out of reach than ever, rarely giving interviews and only making appearances on television for advertising campaigns. Although Kate's image seemed to be everywhere, few members of the public had ever heard her speak.

One of Kate's first assignments after leaving rehab was being interviewed for *Dazed and Confused* by the magazine's co-founder, Jefferson

Hack, who asked, 'There's been a lot of different men mentioned in your life recently, but no one permanent relationship? Is there no one out there good enough for you?'

By early 2001 Kate and Jefferson were inseparable, attending film festivals in Berlin and Cannes and escaping to her recently purchased house in the country near Marlowe in Buckinghamshire. Now one of fashion's alpha couples, she sat with Jefferson in the front row at the autumn/winter 2001 shows in Paris, saying, 'I'm just enjoying the shows and shopping; it's nice for a change.'

Her hair was now in its shortest cut yet, and perhaps to soften the effect of the chic gamine crop her new make-up essential was 'cream blusher and bronzer'. By the end of the year her beauty obsession would be 'hair extensions' and as for the crop: 'Never again. I had to do it because I'd talked about it for years, but now I'm growing it long again.' Soon Kate could be seen sporting mannish trilbies and flat caps, popularising hats for the first time in years.

Up until this point, Kate had largely favoured vintage, rather than modern, designer clothes. Now part of the fashion establishment with Jefferson, her wardrobe was becoming more of the moment; more labelly. She wore a Chloe dress from Stella McCartney's final collection to watch the show. But she was also aware of new designers like Brit posh-punk Luella Bartley, whose label was then in its third season, as well as the newly cool Balenciaga, a label with which she was so enamoured that she approached designer Nicolas Ghesquiere to ask if she could model in his spring 2001 show.

After the show Kate was given free clothes ('I've got so much Balenciaga, but it's never enough'), as well as a leather bag, one of the first Ghesquiere had designed for the house. It was one of a very limited edition because of a production error, and consequently the bag didn't even yet have a name. Kate was photographed carrying it around town and within a matter of weeks the fashion world was clamouring to know where to buy Kate's bag. 'At that point, we realised without a doubt, her influence is enormous and global,' said Ghesquiere. The freshly christened Lariat bag went on to become one of the most successful 'It' bags of the 2000s.

Kate's approach to luxury is fun rather than flashy. She has nice things, but has never worn logo-laden accessories. Kate doesn't care about looking rich. Sophisticated, yes; glamorous in her own way, but never flash.

Her favourite new possession at this time was a

London, 2002.

'Kate borrowed this dress after a *Harpers Bazaar* photoshoot. I think it says she liked the dress. She looked great in it. Kate never wears things that she doesn't like so I took it as a compliment rather than as a testimony to her spontaneity.' TOM FORD

London, 2001.

brown leather suitcase by Asprey, a gift from the label's creative director David Tang who she had recently met on a trip to India to study meditation. The bespoke luggage bore the legend DIVA embossed in discreet gold lettering under the handle; inside were the words KATE MOSS. DO NOT TOUCH. It was indeed diva luggage; the kind of case that should be rolled up the gang-plank ramp of a cruise liner in the 1930s.

It is all part of the Moss mystique that it is impossible to work out how much she's paid for any piece. By now she was a multi-millionairess, her personal wealth an estimated £15 million, but in contrast to the 2000s new bling generation led by Jennifer Lopez and Puff Daddy, her style was not about wearing her wealth. Kate still just wanted to look cool.

Her touches of luxury were old school; antique jewellery, vintage furs, a sky blue convertible Mercedes 280SL from the early 1970s. But her everyday accessories are discreetly deluxe; a python purse and diary by Smythson. Her 'desert island essentials' would be 'a Hermes blanket and a tuberose candle' … and a Rolling Stones album.

Kate's views had clearly moved on from her declaration a decade earlier: 'I wouldn't wear fur.' Vintage dealer Keni Valenti says, 'I think she definitely makes fur seem modern; not like the 1980s…'

Perhaps it was because her approach to wearing fur was more about rock 'n' roll rebellion than rich bitch flashiness. When asked who her fashion hero is, Kate name-checks Janis Joplin, the maverick blues-singing hippy whose boho mix of vests and waistcoats and jangly jewellery is reminiscent of what Marianne Faithfull describes as Anita Pallenberg's 'evil glamour'.

'There's a legacy going on there,' observes Joliffe of Anita's fashion influence on Kate. 'It's so old school; Anita's been doing it for forty years. It's an amoral kind of style; it's not about wanting to be liked, it's about being really f-ing stylish.'

Certainly, this seemed to be Kate's approach. 'I wear what I want to wear,' she told reporters asking about her fur stole, believed to be made by Luella Bartley from vintage tails for the YSL Rive Gauche store opening in February 2002. Worn with dark skinny jeans and a simple black top, the look was pure Kate: scruffily glamorous.

'You don't see a lot of famous people [vintage shopping],' says Ihenacho. 'I love rummaging, but some people don't have the patience. She's like a kid in the sweet shop; she wants to see what's at the bottom of the pile.'

'Kate Moss pioneered the vintage trend,' says Rellik's Steven Phillips. 'She was one of the first to realise she couldn't get what she wanted from current designers and brands, so she turned to vintage. And now look at it; the mass market is saturated with the idea.'

The pirate boots reappeared in a Vogue photoshoot in December 2001, worn with an original 1920s sequinned flapper from Virginia's, shot by Corinne Day. While she was styled for the shoot, the look was unmistakably Kate's; a rare blurring of her professional and personal images.

'Who else would have put a pair of tatty pirate boots with a little sequin dress?' says Virginia Bates. 'It's just so cool. In those days anyone else would have worn a pair of strappy diamante Gina shoes. She's very ironic and that is what we love; the hard and the soft, the delicate sequinned tulle dress, and then a pair of boots. I love that look. That's about having the confidence to do it. Chutzpah. She's got chutzpah.'

When the magazine hit the news stands, 'That was it – everybody wanted a sequinned dress. It was no longer fancy dress; it became chic.' Kate was once again blurring the boundaries between eveningwear and daywear.

'I still regret letting this Vivienne Westwood "Marilyn Monroe P***" T-shirt dress go. Another vintage dealer persuaded me to part with it, and then I immediately saw it on Kate. It's a really offensive piece, but it's so rare. But I think it ended up in the right place: it's saying you have to take the p*** out of celebrity. So this T-shirt needed to be with someone who could express that thought. And who better than Kate?'
TRACEY TOLKIEN, STEINBERG & TOLKIEN VINTAGE, LONDON

'Anita Pallenberg always came here, and one day she called and said "I've got someone wondeful for you" and Kate stomped through the door one day. She was just about to go out in Fulham to see Jesse Woods performing. She bought white 1950s woven shoes, an orange Courreges jumper, a Vivienne Westwood rare leather mini. And she wore it all out that night.'
JEFF IHENACHO, ONE OF A KIND VINTAGE, LONDON

She would still throw on the slip dress that Galliano gave her for her twenty-first 'in the garden at my house in the country when I want to feel glamorous', a decadently laid-back approach to luxury that seems very F. Scott Fitzgerald. She loved the recently released movie *Gosford Park*, and wished she could have lived in the 1920s.

'She's got that British spirit that only a British girl can have,' says Burberry designer Christopher Bailey. 'She's able to have that real elegance, but it's always a thrown-together casual elegance. You never feel like she's studied herself too much and she hasn't; she's got very natural style – effortless.'

Kate became the new face of Burberry, the slick black and white Mario Testino photographs giving the very proper British brand a new edgy appeal. 'Kate Moss is very much a Londoner,' says Bailey, 'very cool and very strong.'

Rimmel also wanted to capitalise on Kate's London cool. The cosmetics brand signed her up to a multimillion-pound contract to star in its advertising campaign uttering the catchphrase 'Get the London look', making Kate synonymous with Britain's style capital. Kate was becoming more British than a cup of tea, literally; she also became the face of the UK Tea Council, claiming to drink 'ten to fifteen cups a day'.

In January 2002, Jefferson and Kate attended an exhibition of Mario Testino's portraits at London's National Portrait Gallery.

Kate's outfit seemed to somehow sum up everything about her current style. The cut-out black dress by Balenciaga was a bare and edgy design; somehow sweet but tough at the same time. She carried an elegant vintage sequinned clutch from Virginia's, worn with Donatella's ruby bracelet, and a wrecked – and therefore totally rock 'n' roll – off-white vintage fur coat. Kate vamped it up for the waiting photographers like never before.

But this was something of a last hurrah. Kate and Jefferson were expecting a baby. 'I was huge when I was pregnant. She was only 6lb, but I carried it all round the front. And my head turned into a basketball.' But she admitted, 'I like being fat for a change.'

Kate wore loose jeans, and Prada tunic tops, furry gilets and pretty white cotton embroidered smocks. Even Kate's cravings were chic: Japanese food. Her wardrobe was dominated by the ultra-wearable: 'This year I like the Marc Jacobs jeans look – denim and [knee] high boots.'

At the National
Portrait Gallery
in London for the
'Mario Testino
Portraits' show,
2002.

London, 2002.

'This off the shoulder dress is by Jean Muir. Its actually orange suede. Jean Muir did a lot of great suede stuff in the early seventies; suits, jackets, some of it had embossed designs in it. This is quite plain. The early seventies Jean Muir pieces were kind of disco. Although this is more of a Halston look, only without the jersey, a heavier version of the Halston style drape.'

TRACEY TOLKIEN,
STEINBERG &
TOLKIEN VINTAGE,
LONDON

'I have actually never met Kate, it was a complete coincidence that she happened to wear one of our dresses! I think she must have bought it from Topshop, (she has since bought many more) but a friend called me one day to say they had seen Kate wearing it, and of course I was delighted. I love the way she looks in Darimeya; so relaxed and bohemian. This is exactly our vibe.'

DARIMEYA, LONDON

Pregnant with Lila,
London 2002.

'She got really casual when she was pregnant,' recalls New York vintage dealer Katy Rodriguez. 'She didn't want to wear heels and so was always [coming in] looking for flat boots.'

In fact, Kate was spending most of her time with her clothes off. She was sitting for a nude portrait for artist Lucien Freud from 7pm to 2am at least three nights a week for eight months. She was only late once, on the morning she found out she was pregnant.

Kate had met Lucien, as she had Jefferson, through an earlier interview with *Dazed and Confused* magazine, during which she had commented, 'I'd like to meet Lucien Freud. I heard he was really cool. Like for an 80-year-old, he's really hip and cool apparently.' The artist got in touch.

Kate described the painter as the most interesting person she'd ever met 'because he's a genius'. The feeling was mutual. Bella Freud, Lucien's daughter claims, 'She really does pay attention to art … She's really interested in everything. She somehow amazingly just doesn't miss stuff. Being her, people will invite her to check things out, so you'll find that she's actually seen all these amazing perform- ances of some incredible ballet … I think, "God, how the hell did she think of doing that?" but then, she's really clever in checking things out.' She says her father adored spending time with Kate, 'largely because of Kate's intelligence and the fact that she's not afraid to say exactly what she thinks.'

At twenty-eight, Kate had matured into a unique individual; widely travelled, well read, with a back catalogue of unique and extraordinary experi- ences. 'She's not really a girl who learned things at school,' says Mario Sorrenti. 'She learned things from life. She is surrounded by the greatest artists, the greatest writers, the greatest fashion designers, the greatest businessmen, and it's from that contact that she takes everything there is to take.'

'She's always reading three or four books at a time,' says James Brown, 'but she learns things very organically, not through reading.' Her reading list at this time was long and varied. Lately, she had been working through Hunter S. Thompson's *Masculine*, and *The World of Suzie Wong*. 'I like books about sex and drugs and rock 'n' roll, really. Henry Miller, Anais Nin.' And most recently, she had been reading a French novel, *Lila Says*, in which the titular character is a teenage Lolita-esque seductress.

In September 2002 Kate gave birth to a daughter, Lila Grace Hack, 'And I had simply the best birth. I had candles and everything. A bottle of Cristal [champagne]. I had the best time.'

Stella McCartney party , June 2002.

In London while pregnant with Lila in 2002.

London, 2002.

# Style 7 Icon

'I've just been to McQueen and got some shorts for Glastonbury. And I'm planning something lamé for Elton's White Tie and Tiara Ball. Jean Harlow hair, don't you think?'
KATE MOSS

Another Magazine
party, New
York, 2003.

ate's first post-pregnancy reappearance was a triumph. She had borrowed a navy satin cocktail dress on a photo-shoot, shredded and embellished with jewels, from the (newly revived) house of Lanvin. Arriving at San Lorenzo for dinner with Jefferson, with her hair scraped back and wearing her signature Mary Janes, she looked radiant. 'The best thing about Kate is that she makes every dress disappear because of her persona; her face is so strong and full of emotion,' says Lanvin designer Alber Elbaz, 'so that whatever she wears doesn't matter. This is her force and her power; we look at her.'

'Kate wore the dress the first night out after her baby girl, and somebody called to tell me, but I said I'm not sure it is my dress, because it's not out yet.
But then Suzy Menkes announced the news [in the *International Herald Tribune*].
When Kate is wearing clothes it becomes her own. She wears it in a way that nobody else does and there is nothing victim about it.
It was a very personal choice, a very bohemian dress, it wasn't a cocktail dress or as the Americans would say an "after five" dress. It was just scarves, panels of fabrics with a necklace stitched to clothes the inspiration was a bolshevicks when they were going into Russia the women were sewing jewellery into clothes so when they were shot not all of them died because the jewels protected them. So this collection was all about protection.
This was a beginning for a new time for Lanvin. Kate made it cool without publicity, without a major campaign, without talkshows. She made it happen and I'm thanking her for being a part of Lanvin, and our family.'
ALBER ELBAZ, LANVIN, PARIS

Kate and Jefferson
leaving San
Lorenzo's in London.

But the dress didn't go unnoticed. Overnight, both Lanvin and Kate were rocketed back into the global spotlight. 'She has this knack of spotting a garment that's of interest,' says Bella Freud. 'She must have seen the Lanvin dress – it was a really extraordinary dress – and just thought "that's it". She set it out there for everyone to follow. But she does it in a particularly effortless way.'

Kate's style choices seemed to have moved beyond merely looking wonderful, to an almost magical prescience. 'Our logo is a mother and daughter,' says Elbaz of the label's illustration, depicting designer Jeanne Lanvin and her daughter Marguerite, 'and I found it more than symbolic that she wore that dress.'

At twenty-nine, in four short months, Kate appeared to have lost all her baby fat. She had been watching what she ate 'a bit ... after having Lila, I couldn't have my French toast in my fry-up in the morning. I had to watch what I was eating, after having been eating for two ... but I didn't make an intensive effort.' She admits to doing yoga, and working out 'a bit' in Thailand on holiday.

But Kate had also been employing a more unorthodox fitness regime. Still a rock chick at heart, one of her earliest post-pregnancy appearances would be pole-dancing in the White Stripes music video for their cover of Burt Bacharach's 'I Just Don't Know What To Do With Myself'.

'I said, "I don't know – how about Kate Moss doing a pole dance?"' the video's director Sofia Coppola recalled. 'I said that because I would like to see it ... The band liked my idea.' Kate had lessons at the Astral strip club. 'It was amazing exercise,' she said. 'We did it for toning as it was more fun than going to the gym. It is so hardcore, pulling your body up onto a pole.'

Kate wasn't compromising her style for motherhood; her nappy bag was a white Hermes Birkin holdall. Lila, equally stylish, got a Dior baby bottle and a leopard-print lined pushchair.

Kate's only concession to practicality was that her shoes were flatter, but no less stylish: strappy sexy Roman sandals or sweet little ballet pumps, worn with a series of spectacularly short dresses. 'What she throws on is so random and yet so right,' says stylist Brana Wolf. '[I remember] suddenly seeing her in a ballet flat, and thinking "that's brilliant".'

The ballet shoes were soon everywhere. Kate managed to make the sweet little pumps look prim, but also somehow cool. 'That's how pumps should be worn,' said French Sole founder Jane Winkworth, whose black Pirouettes pumps Kate had been wearing. 'They're supposed to be indolent and sexy, slopped down a bit at the back and a bit scuffed up from where you've whipped them off and stuffed them in your handbag.'

Having spent her maternity months in jeans and tunic tops, Kate's new obsession was dresses, which she indulged in sometimes unexpected locales. In February, she attended the NME awards in Hammersmith to present The Clash with a Godlike Genius Award, alongside her friend Bobby Gillespie of the band Primal Scream.

Bands like the Sugababes wore the regulation issue pop uniform; low cut jeans, heavily customised T-shirts and fluorescent belts. Kate, her hair twisted elegantly back off her face, had her own dress code. She was wearing a strapless, wide-skirted prom dress, pleated into broad black and white stripes, with spike heels and black opaque tights.

'She revived that 1950s thing; demure 1950s dresses and fur coats,' says vintage dealer Tracey Tolkien. 'She went through different phases, she gravitated towards 1950s day dresses, with the bodices and flared skirts; those suited her very well. But then she also liked punk stuff. Of all of our customers she just has this instinct of what suits her and what's different from what other people are wearing.'

'She'll suddenly wear some grand dress, something very classic or very 1950s that you'd never imagine her in,' says Bella Freud. 'Most people think, "This is what suits me; I'm only going to wear this." But she wears it, because she's not just one genre; she's out there, as an innovator, in dressing for herself. She's interested in what hasn't been done yet.'

Part of the appeal of Kate's new look was making even the dressiest dresses seem somehow accessible. Lanvin's Alber Elbaz recalls of his cocktail dress, 'The way she wore it, there was something she did; she wore it a bit open, she didn't zip it up all the way, so it was very nonchalant. And that's what she does; she takes the high-end preciousness and makes it real and that's what we love.'

'She does love that sweet dress look,' says designer Sue Stemp, whose yellow 1950s-style dress Kate wore for her thirtieth birthday lunch, 'but then she's always going to wear it with a killer heel that's going to knock it in a different direction; it's really the juxtaposition. She's just a great stylist, the way she mixes things up always looks new and fresh and different.'

Kate's hair had grown back. Longer and more

NME Carling
Awards, 2003.

Arriving at *The Gentle Birth Method* book launch, 2004.

tousled than ever, it was starting to look like Kate's ultimate style statement. 'Her hair always looks the same,' says Susie Crippen of J Brand. 'It's not overdone, it's always tousled, always attainable. And that gives her a naturalness that was around in the 1960s and 1970s – between the 1950s when everything was groomed and then the 1980s where everything was so solid. It lends an air of breeziness to her. Still with a casual elegance though, but attainable; you look and think, "I can do that!"'

Kate's ability to dress for occasions was being challenged to its limits. 'I remember her chatting with Sam Taylor-Wood about what to wear for going to the Palace,' says Bella Freud, 'and I knew she wasn't going to be constrained; she'd use it as a way of doing something really witty.'

Kate had been invited to Buckingham Palace to meet the Queen, who was greeting Britain's 'women of achievement', including Sam Taylor-Wood, J. K. Rowling and Charlotte Church.

On the morning of the event, Taylor-Wood panicked over her original choice of an Alexander McQueen dress, begging Kate to race over to her house with a suitcase of clothes to borrow.

Kate, of course, had already chosen her own outfit. 'She is always pitch-perfect in these things,' recalls Taylor-Wood (who eventually chose Kate's silver satin Chanel dress and a black Chanel jacket). 'She wore a kind of vintage royal-blue dress.'

Kate's choice was so perfect that it was almost a faux pas: '[It was] the same colour as the Queen's,' says Taylor-Wood. Kate had also shrugged on a short white vintage fur jacket, which was equally evocative of royalty, and somehow had the same spirit as Vivienne Westwood's irreverent renditions of the monarchy's motifs: tiny crowns and mini coronation capelets.

'Kate gets the playfulness and naughtiness of stylishness,' says stylist and *Cheap Date* editor Kira Jolliffe. 'Its about understanding rock and roll, and using that to meet the Queen.'

Kate's reinvention of the dress reached its zenith with a yellow chiffon ruched prom dress that she wore for *Another* magazine's party in honour of Gwyneth Paltrow in New York.

Kate wore it again for Lila's christening, held near her house in the country. 'She had on something like a pale-yellow … 1950s-style dress, you know, with a strapless bodice and then a chiffon skirt, like to just below the knee … like a real lady dress,' remembers Bella Freud, who recalls feeling amazed that Kate was able to look so 'fresh' one afternoon so soon after she had given birth to Lila.

The lemon yellow prom dress, and the Lanvin cocktail dress, ignited a revival of interest in The Dress, not as sexy eveningwear but as a way of dressing for day that was unapologetically girly. 'Kate can look traditionally feminine,' says Charlie Brear of the Vintage Wedding Dress company, who has styled Kate for the Rimmel advertisements, 'but she always looks like a gorgeous woman; that's what makes her a modern trendsetting icon. And she's got amazing legs – they're always out.'

This was a period when Kate was arguably moving into the peak of her powers as a style icon. Years later, Cameron Silver of LA vintage store Decades would comment, 'There are three items that my customers all come in with photos of Kate asking for: the yellow ruched prom dress, the leopard print vintage fur coat from the early 1960s, and the black long fur jacket. Those are three looks that have always been very attractive to our customers.'

As Silver points out, 'Those three pieces are really strong statement pieces: a spotted jacket, a gothy, rocky jacket, the strength of that lemon yellow dress.' These were hard-won pieces. 'She's not a lazy shopper,' says Silver, 'she's very proactive. And she really does it herself, it's not a stylist.'

In an age when celebrity stylists were becoming commonplace, Kate's passion for shopping was starting to seem almost idiosyncratic. 'She's risen above that whole thing of other people doing things for her; I don't think anyone else [celebrity] does that,' says Brear. 'She's in there, sourcing from source like a stylist.'

Brear knows that 'as a stylist, your biggest talent is you can go into a charity shop and be there for two minutes and know what's in there. It's about having that hawk-like eye, [to see] that one thing in the whole shop that you can make something out of. She loves a bargain as much as the next girl, and always finds the treasure in a pile of junk. That's why she has that knack, and that's why she's got that style icon status.'

Shopping in this way, and in particular in vintage stores, meant that Kate's wardrobe was made up of distinctive individual pieces. Any piece in her wardrobe had made it in there purely on its own merits, not because it was that season's colour, but because it was a fabulous example of a garment in its own right.

'What makes Kate so brilliant is that she is not constricted by any sort of notions of fashion, of what's "in" or "out",' says Bella Freud. 'She seems to choose something, not on whether it's a cool thing or not a cool thing, but because its just one thing, that for just for one moment fits a mood that's going on, just with her.'

'Kate's so assured in her style,' says Jarred Cairns from Decades. 'Everything looks great on her. [But] even if people around her were saying, "Um, we're not sure," her personal taste just overrides that … and she knows. I mean, she's worn so many clothes.'

Styling herself has become so instinctive that occasionally she'll end up doing it on photoshoots too. 'She'll say, "Why don't I wear this silver belt, because it's just so cool," and usually she's right,' says *Vanity Fair* contributing stylist Sarajane Hoare. Because who knows better than Kate what looks good on Kate?

'She is very quick to get dressed,' says Tom Ford. 'I remember Kate at Stella McCartney's wedding in Scotland. We were staying in the same hotel. Kate would have bed hair, no make-up and be wearing a robe. Everyone else would have been getting ready for hours. Then Kate would disappear back into her room and come out twenty minutes later with her hair done, make-up on and wearing the most beautiful outfit.'

Consequently, 'there are a million images of Kate looking amazing,' says Matthew Williamson, who claims Kate's greatest talent is 'dressing so appropriately for occasions. She straddles being chic, elegant, cool, urban and streetwise.'

And so, when Kate dressed to meet friends for tea at Claridges, she wore a ladylike black and white outfit; prim heels, a neat little skirt and a

Leaving the Groucho Club, London, 2003.

Arriving at the V&A Museum.

cashmere sweater. The sweater bore the hand-written legend, 'Ginsberg is God'.

'She always looks at ease in what she's wearing,' says stylist Brana Wolf. 'Women know how hard that is. The average woman spends a lot of time trying to pull an outfit together, and then not feeling so comfortable. It's an effortlessness that her outfits portray. People feel that about her when they see that image; to be able to throw on a few clothes and look that fabulous.'

Bella Freud had designed the jumper, and also the slogan, and insists, 'Kate got the joke. She's got the most incredible sense of humour; she gets the subtlety of things. The conversation around her is always so funny and irreverent. She's so bright, but she keeps it to herself. She doesn't make a big thing about it. She doesn't try to edit herself, and the things she likes.'

As to Ginsberg, 'I think Jefferson got her into him; he is really interested in culture and writers and poets. She likes that certain people are good conduits for [things like] that. Jefferson was really great at saying, "Have you seen this photo, or this book?" A great person to show you things. He's like that. [He's] amazingly interesting.'

Kate's love of 'thrifting' (as vintage shopping was now starting to be called thanks to thrifting fanzine *Cheap Date*) was showcased in a photoshoot in British *Vogue*'s May issue.

The idea had come from *Vogue*'s new contributing editor and *Cheap Date* co-founder Bay Garnett. The shoot took place at Kate's house, photographed by her friend Juergen Teller. Garnett's co-stylist was Anita Pallenberg.

30th birthday,
Claridges Hotel, 2004.

'I just happened to be in London, and I was just flicking though the paper and I saw the pictures of Kate, and I thought "no, it can't be"... but it is the same dress. I bought it for *The Man With the Golden Gun* premiere in 1973, from [vintage store] Antiquarius on the Kings Road. It's probably from the 1920s or 1930s. The next time I wore it was with Rod Stewart, in 1975, to Cubby Broccoli's New Year's Eve party in Beverly Hills.

In 1992, I sold it to a vintage dealer, and I never saw or heard anything of it again until I saw it on Kate.

It's bias cut, and incredibly heavy. It's covered in blue-black sequins, sewn like fish scales, so they shimmered. It just catches the light. It has a very low V, so you can see a lot of décolletage, and it's almost glued to the body because of the weight; like a mermaid. So you had to be very small and have no chest to wear it. And that's the sort of figure women had back in the 1920s and 1930s; very boyish. If they were going out to dinner at the Savoy or wherever, that is what they would have worn.

She obviously wanted something very unusual, and different. Maybe she could have found something equally beautiful, but not that unique. That's certainly what appealed to me about the dress, and it must have been what appealed to her.

I doubt she could have found anything like that anywhere else... they don't make dresses that spectacular any more.

And I loved the way she wore the dress, so I sent her a little note saying that...'

BRITT EKLAND, ACTRESS, NEW YORK

'IT WAS REALLY HOT,
IT WAS ONE OF THOSE
SUMMERS. THAT WAS
ONE OUR MOST AMAZING
WEEKENDS EVER. WE
WERE STAYING IN THIS
WINNEBAGO BACKSTAGE
(AT GLASTONBURY).
AND IN IT WE HAD ALL
THESE LOOKS IN THERE,
ALL THESE OUTFITS. AND
THE WHOLE WINNEBAGO
WAS FULL OF ROCK AND
ROLL CLOTHES. AND WE
KEPT DOING ANOTHER
OUTFIT, GOING TO SEE A
GIG, GETTING CHANGED
AGAIN, GOING TO
SOMETHING ELSE. WE
DID MORE LOOKS IN
THAT WEEKEND THAN
WE'VE EVER DONE.'
Fran Cutler, friend, London

'Kate can make the ugliest thing
look amazing. Who would have
thought that moccasin knee high
boots could come back in fashion?'
KELLY OSBOURNE,
FRIEND, LONDON

'I came over from New York for Kate's birthday. I took a bag full of a load of clothes I'd recently designed: I was going to choose what to wear when I got there. As soon as James Brown spotted this dress he pulled it out of my bag and said "Kate would love this". And she just popped it on. She looked fantastic in it. I was stunned: there were boxes cluttering up the hallway, with clothes from designers from all over the world. But I think she's just so impulsive.' SUE STEMP, FASHION DESIGNER, NEW YORK

30th birthday, January 16th 200

132

'JEFFREY PATTY OWNER OF NEW YORK VINTAGE STORE SOUTHPAW GAVE KATE THE DRESS FOR HER BIRTHDAY. IT'S BY A 1950S AMERICAN FASHION DESIGNER, CEIL CHAPMAN. WE DIDN'T REALISE, BUT KATE ENDED UP WEARING IT TO MEET THE QUEEN. AND THE QUEEN WAS WEARING EXACTLY THE SAME COLOUR.' Farah Pidgeon, Southpaw Vintage, New York

'Women of Achievment' reception, Buckingham Palace, March 2004.

# 8
# With the
# Band

'I like old-fashioned things. I like reading
Fitzgerald, Oscar Wilde, Evelyn Waugh,
all those classics. And then, I just
like rock 'n' roll really. Old or new.'
KATE MOSS

Isle of Wight
festival,
June 2006.

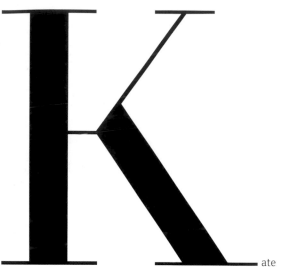

**K**ate had discovered rock style before she discovered rock music. When she was just eleven, her father had given her a poster of David Bowie, dressed as his glam rock alter-ego Aladdin Sane. She liked the look, but didn't hear any of Bowie's music until years later, when tracks like 'Life on Mars', 'Rock & Roll Suicide' and 'Golden Years' would become lifelong favourites.

By now, Kate's closest friends were Hall of Fame legends and their various entourages, from the Rolling Stones to The Beatles, to The Clash and Iggy Pop. But she also hung out with the new generation of bands, from Oasis to Primal Scream, the Happy Mondays and Marilyn Manson. She has a passion for live music. Other models may make rare appearances in the VIP area backstage at stadium concerts, but it's Kate who would pay to see an up-and-coming band play a gig in a dingy back room in a Camden pub, or head off in the rain and the mud to England's summer music festivals year after year.

'Kate is the type who will say she's going to see a group I've never heard of,' says Alexander McQueen, 'and then some weeks later, it'll be the must-know group. She goes to really normal places and she doesn't expect any special treatment.' He recalls a time recently when 'she was going to see an indie group in Islington with Liv Tyler. She loves doing things like that.'

The light blue bathroom at Kate's London home was lined with a photo gallery of rock gods: Sid Vicious, he Rolling Stones, David Bowie. She hung out at Ronnie and Jo Wood's London house, and loved playing dress-up in the attic where they have stored all their old clothes from the late

Babyshambles concert, Florence, Italy, October 2006

Isle of Wight
Festival,
June 2005.

'This sequinned jacket is a precious and expensive 1920s piece. She never minds mixing vintage and cheap; this is a very serious vintage piece, it could have been from Chanel from that period. Now she's combining it with skinny jeans, a wonderful collage of different looks. I think it's okay lthat she's wearing it at the festivall. In the 1920s can you imagine where they were going? They were running around in jazz clubs smoking pot, I bet the clothes got as much of an outing then, some of them were going to things that were wilder than we can imagine.'
TRACEY TOLKIEN, STEINBERG & TOLKIEN VINTAGE, LONDON

'I WAS STANDING AROUND BACKSTAGE AT GLASTONBURY AND SAW ALL THE PAPARAZZI GOING MAD AND I THOUGHT "WHO ARE THEY PAPPING?" AND I TURNED ROUND, AND IT WAS KATE. I SAID "CAN I GIVE YOU AN ALL SAINTS BELT?" AND SHE SAID "SURE, HOW MUCH ARE THEY?" I SAID THEY WERE FREE BUT WE WANTED TO TAKE HER PICTURE IN IT. SHE LOOKED QUITE ORDINARY, BUT WHEN SHE PUT THE BELT ON AND POSED, SHE TRANSFORMED. WHEN SHE DOES HER POSE, YOU SUDDENLY SEE THIS SPARKLE, AND THEN IT WAS LIKE, "AH THERE'S KATE MOSS!" SHE KIND OF JUST POPPED THE BELT ON, IT WAS A LITTLE SLAPDASH, IT WASN'T THROUGH THE BELT LOOPS OR ANYTHING, AND THE BELT END WAS LEFT HANGING. SHE JUST PUT IT ON HER HIPS. SHE WORE IT NON-STOP. I SAW HER LAST YEAR AT GLASTONBURY IN 2007, AND SHE SAID, "I'VE STILL GOT THAT BELT, IT'S WITH ME NOW!" SHE BECAME THE POSTER GIRL FOR FESTIVALS WEARING THAT BELT, IT'S ALL ABOUT THAT MOMENT IN TIME.'
Tahirah Conliffe, Black Betty PR, London

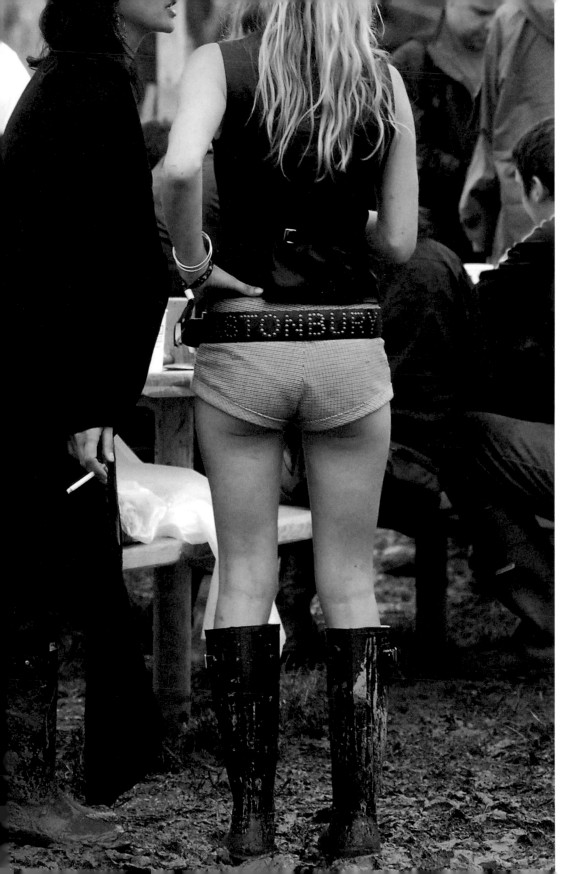

Glastonbury,
2005.

London,
August 2005.

Notting Hill,
London,
May 2005.

1970s. 'We enjoy trying things on. She adores my attic,' says Jo.

She might be the ultimate modern rock chick, but it's not just a pose; Kate knows her music. Ronnie Wood describes her as 'my favourite DJ; when we're at hers, she plays music that blows you away. That could be Frank Sinatra to Mozart then onto the Stones. But it's always incredible. I'm always saying, "I didn't know you knew [about] that!" She's got an incredible taste in music.' Make no mistake, Kate loves rock 'n' roll. In 2005, her soundtrack included Arctic Monkeys, Janis Joplin, Patti Smith and the Rolling Stones.

And so it somehow made sense when Kate fell for Babyshambles front man Pete Doherty. Within days of meeting Kate at her glam-rock themed thirty-first birthday in the Cotswolds, the songwriter had the letter K tattooed on his arm, inside an existing tattoo of a heart.

Pete was not the first musician Kate had linked with. She had previously been spotted with Evan Dando of the Lemonheads, Spacehog's Antony Langdon and Jesse Wood, son of Ronnie, a guitar player whose various bands Kate had been to watch.

Barely a week after their first meeting, Pete appeared on television professing, 'I've really found love with Kate. I think it will last. She's good for me because she's got a beautiful soul and I think I can trust her. I think I can believe her when she says she loves me and I know I mean it when I say I love her.' Overnight, Kate's private life had become access all areas.

Doherty's notoriety fascinated the press and he

Arriving at Cirpriani, London, August 2005.

in turn seemed to bask in the blaze of publicity; good or bad. No stranger to the courtroom, Pete would turn up and chat politely with the reporters, or sit strumming on his guitar, charming his ever-present fans.

That February he was jailed for ten days after being arrested on robbery and blackmail charges, unable to produce the necessary bail. Kate briefly distanced herself, but seemed to find him hard to resist.

A tortured poet, petty thief and drug addict, Pete was a shambling figure, strangely old-fashioned in appearance; moon-faced and pale with wide soulful eyes. A talented lyricist, he was fascinated by 1960s comedian Tony Hancock, whose quaintly dated turns of phrase he quoted in songs like 'Up the Junction', by his previous band The Libertines.

Next to Kate, five years older and considerably more glamorous in tiny shorts, knee-high boots and a mane of peroxide-gold hair, they made an unlikely couple. Kate was playing up her bad-girl image, and was soon partying all night with Pete, but still emerging looking fresh as a daisy each morning.

The contrasts in Kate's lifestyle were growing more pronounced than ever before. On 6 June 2005, Kate flew to New York to receive the prestigious CDFA (Council of Fashion Designers of America)'s Award for Fashion Influence; the style equivalent of an Oscar. 'She dresses in a way that means something,' says Peter Arnold, CDFA Executive Director.

CFDA Fashion Awards, 2005.

Kate accepted her award wearing a stunning ballet pink strapless corset dress overlaid in black lace, designed by her old friend John Galliano for Dior Couture, worn with her favourite Westwood Sex shoes, rootsy bleached hair and her signature black eyeliner. To live up to her award, Kate's look that night consequently inspired Galliano's entire spring/summer ready-to-wear collection for Dior.

Three weeks later Kate was at Glastonbury, wearing mud-spattered Hunter wellies and hot pants, with rats-tail hair, her gold lurex tunic top clinging to her body as the rain poured down while she hung onto a pint, a cigarette and Pete. (And, somewhat improbably, a Dior monogrammed mini-holdall, which she pulled from the back of the chauffeur-driven Land Rover she arrived in. Even knee-deep in mud, Kate travelled in style.)

Proof that Kate can make anything fashionable, the Hunter rubber rainboots instantly sold out across the country.

Since Kate's stylish appearance at the festival the previous summer, she had become synonymous with rock chic. Her iconic look this year centred around a studded belt that spelt out the legend Glastonbury Rocks, worn with a waistcoat and checked hot pants: a kind of abbreviated rock suit, accessorised with the ever-present Hunters.

But Kate was also upping the ante, bringing glam-rock to Glastonbury with layers of gold sparkly clothing, from a beaded vintage top (with hot pants and wellies) to a sequinned shrug, a metallic gold ribbed cardigan and the lurex tunic. 'She's a self-confessed magpie,' says stylist and vintage dealer Charlie Brear. 'She loves anything with a bit of sparkle.'

Later that summer, Pete performed a duet with Elton John for Live 8. Dressed in a military jacket, white T-shirt and skinny jeans, accessorised with a skinny pink scarf and catwalk eye make-up, Pete stumbled through T-Rex's 'Children of the Revolution'.

Just as Anita Pallenberg influenced Keith Richard's rock style in the 1960s; (all those effeminate glam-rock touches – the scarves, the bangles, the velvet shirts – came from Keith rummaging in her wardrobe), so Kate and Pete's style became more interchangeable: skinny jeans, rosary beads, waistcoats and trilbies, very-Hendrix military jackets, frock coats and peaked caps.

But Pete already had his own style credentials. Dior Homme designer Hedi Slimane had already been photographing Pete on tour and at home for his book *London: Birth of a Cult*, long before he had started dating Kate. References to Doherty's distinctive look – skinny drainpipe trousers and braces – showed up in his Dior Homme catwalk show in Paris that summer.

Kate's friends looked on and wondered about the ill-starred lovers. 'She seems to have embraced this myth of the rock 'n' roll life,' said the designer Anna Sui. David Tang observed, 'They're living on the edge, and that's what they want. It's in defiance of something. I don't understand it, but they find it incredibly romantic. Like Bonnie and Clyde.'

Doherty and Kate had plenty in common. She was reading Oscar Wilde's *De Profundis*. He was also reading the complete works of Oscar

Wilde, and referenced the Romantic poets, Emily Dickinson and Baudelaire as influences. For years he kept diaries in a series of notebooks he calls The Books of Albion, containing song lyrics and sketches, old love letters and wine stains and, more recently, 'Kate' scrawled in Pete's own blood; it was a very rock and roll romance.

'I like old-fashioned things,' says Kate. 'I like reading Fitzgerald, Oscar Wilde, Evelyn Waugh, all those classics. And then, I just like rock 'n' roll really. Old or new.' They both loved music from the 1960s and 1970s: The Clash; the Buzzcocks. Along with her rock chick wardrobe, she was wearing romantic, pretty perfumes; 1930s classic L'Heure Bleue by Guerlain, and Bluebell by Penhaligon's; the scent of rainy English forests.

Doherty was also something of a romantic. Leslie Verrinder of vintage store Tin Tin Collectibles recalls, 'Pete Doherty came in the day before Valentine's day; he bought some 1930s cocktail sticks, a pretty comb, a bakelite bangle, a diamante brooch; a little 1950s thing. He pulled out some balled-up notes. He came out [of Alfie's market] with about six bags ... actually I think he was thrown out.'

Marianne Faithfull had her rock 'n' roll scandal. (She was arrested naked, but for a fur rug, during an infamous police raid on a Rolling Stones party in 1967.) Anita had hers (Keith Richards' 1977 heroin bust in Canada). Kate's fatal attraction was Pete Doherty, and this nearly proved to be her downfall.

On 15 September 2005 the *Mirror* newspaper published a front-page story allegedly showing grainy video stills of Kate using cocaine in a recording studio in London. The morning the story broke, Kate was away in New York being shot by Mario Sorrenti for an issue of French *Vogue* that she was to guest edit.

The story exploded worldwide. Kate found herself under siege in Manhattan by the press, and photographs of her, simply but stylishly dressed in a black cotton jersey slip dress, ballet pumps and huge incognito sunglasses were circulated worldwide. Even in the midst of a crisis, Kate still looked infuriatingly cool; a chunky gold chain necklace perfectly coordinated with the gold chain handle of her Marc Jacobs bag.

As many of her million-dollar advertising contracts started to melt away, Kate issued a public apology, and checked into rehab in Arizona.

But Kate's closest fashion friends rallied round. At the end of his ready-to-wear show in Paris the following month, Alexander McQueen walked the catwalk in a T-shirt bearing the slogan 'We Love You, Kate'.

Kate reappeared four weeks later: first, at a party to launch her special edition of Paris *Vogue*, also something of a homecoming. She wore a sweet, sleeveless pleated cocktail dress by Lanvin in scarlet red. 'They say that a picture ... paints a thousand words,' says Alber Elbaz of the demure yet somehow defiant choice of dress. 'I think that when Kate is wearing clothes, it's not about the dress. It's about her.'

'For me the scandal is over,' declared Paris *Vogue* editor, Carine Roitfeld. 'This is the new Kate and, finally, she's healthier and has come back stronger.'

Glastonbury
festival, 2005

'THIS IS A VICTORIAN MOURNING CAPE MADE OF LACE AND VELVET, WITH JET BEADING, FROM OUR LONDON STORE. IT WAS JUST SUCH A COMPLETE SURPRISE WHEN I SAW HER IN THE NEWSPAPER WEARING IT AT GLASTONBURY. I WONDER, WHAT DREW HER TO THAT? MOST PEOPLE WHO BUY VICTORIAN CLOTHES ARE GOTHS. AND I WOULD NOT SAY THAT KATE WAS GOTH. IT'S FLEETWOOD MAC MEETS (VELVET UNDERGROUND SINGER) NICO, IT'S SORT OF THE GOTH ROMANTIC WAREHOUSE LOOK; WHICH NOONE HAS EVER COMBINED UP TO THIS POINT AND PROBABLY WILL NEVER BE ABLE TO AGAIN. HOW COULD ANYONE CONNECT PVC JEANS, A STUDDED BELT AND PEOPLE WHO HAVE TO WEAR CAPES BECAUSE THEIR HUSBAND IS DEAD? IT'S A VERY STRANGE BREW. BUT IT WORKS.'

Tracey Tolkien, Steinberg & Tolkien vintage, London

Right: Glastonbury
festival, 2006.

Below: Babyshambles
concert, Florence,
Italy, October 2006.

Wireless Festival,
Hyde Park,
London, June 2006.

Right: Outside
friend Davinia
Taylor's house
in London,
February 2006.

dealer Tracy Tolkien. 'She was our biggest cape
buyer; we'd put them aside saying, "Kate would
like that".' Capes seemed to be Kate's latest
obsession; from embellished vintage capes to a
beige fake fur style, and an Alexander McQueen
version in black leather.

Kate appeared on stage with Pete, for the
Babyshambles track 'La Belle et la Bete', singing
the lyric 'Is she more beautiful than me?' In the
late afternoon sun Kate cast a dramatic image;
'The fallen angel,' says stylist Charlie Brear. 'That's
iconic too; that's another side of her being a style
icon, as well as being top of the tree. She does the
rock 'n' roll thing incredibly well. Not giving a
damn; that's the most attractive thing about her.'

Not giving a damn was starting to be symbolised
by Kate's new addiction: hot pants. She was rarely
seen out of shorts all summer, from her trusty
Diesel denim hot pants, to her Topshop black
zip-up mini all-in-one, or tailored shorts for tea at
the Dorchester.

For the wedding of her friends, stylist Katy
England and Primal Scream's Bobby Gillespie, Kate
cut down the legs of an Ossie Clark trouser suit
to create an unconventional but chic hot-pant
suit, which she wore with a straw trilby and
platform sandals.

Kate suddenly started wearing something she'd
never worn before: the same thing, day after day
… an endless succession of the same vests and
waistcoats with shorts or skinny jeans and ballet
flats. Asked how many pairs of jeans she owned,
she replied 'a lot'.

In London with James Brown.

'The high-waisted jeans in that picture were in the Ghost show and James Brown, who was just watching the show, came backstage afterwards and said Kate would love them. So we gave them to him to show her and indeed she did love them, wore them that night, was photographed to death in them and started a whole new trend immediately. She looked so fab – she's the perfect person to wear them. They were one of the first high-waisted denim styles at the time. It was a completely new look for denim which fitted perfectly with her original style; she brought her own unique style to them.'

TANYA SARNE,
GHOST, LONDON

'SHE JUST FOUND IT IN THE SHOP ONE DAY... SHE'S TRULY A FASHION ICON... EVEN THOUGH IT'S A BIG SIZE IT REALLY WORKS ON HER SMALL FRAME. SHE'S JUST ONE OF THOSE ECLECTIC DRESSERS, AND SOMEHOW IT JUST COMES OUT WORKING LIKE A DREAM.'

Jeff Ihenacho, One of a Kind Vintage, London

Attending the wedding
of make up artist
and friend Charlotte
Tilbury, Ibiza,
September 2006.

Her beauty routine was similarly laid-back. 'I just wash my face! Wash my hair. I don't do anything special, just what everyone else does.' Even for a night out, 'shower, a bit of eyeliner, and I'm out the door'. Which is just as well, because Kate was off on tour.

And Kate had packed the perfect hippy rocker wardrobe; appearing with Babyshambles on stage in Dublin in a new Biba shorts 'playsuit' with balloon sleeves and tiny buttons given to her by Biba's new designer Bella Freud. 'Kate loves the tunics and the playsuits – and they're almost the same vibe as 30 years ago.' And Kate knew, because Anita Pallenberg had also passed an original Biba playsuit on to her.

She stayed on tour as the band moved on to the next dates in Florence. Quite justifiably, when the new issue of *Pop* magazine asked Kate to 'describe what you do', she replied, 'I rock and roll.'

After returning from a New Year's holiday in Thailand Pete moved in with Kate (he had been thrown out of his East End flat owing £10,000 rent, and further costs for the graffitied walls and miscellaneous criminal damages).

The pair would escape at the weekends and lark around for photographers as they skipped down a country lane together in the Cotswolds, Kate in wellies, white jeans and a fur coat. And in March 2007, wearing a parka coat with matted hair while driving her car in the Cotswolds, Pete seemed to have achieved the impossible, making her not care about her appearance.

'In the country, I've got a whole room. I was

'It's a very pretty dress, with little flowers. I think she must have cut it though, because I remember it being longer. The dress is by a designer called Will Hemmik, but I don't think she knew who the designer was. It's certainly not a designer I've come across before, anyway. Though we do have another couple of pieces by him in the shop. She didn't seem to be looking for anything specific, she just liked the colour and the pattern, and the shape of the dress. It is such a signature part of her look, the floral dresses, which is why they did them for the Topshop range, I suppose. But she's been wearing them for years. And she looks gorgeous in them. It is interesting that she wears these little floral dresses, and she'll cut them up and wear them with little shoes, but then she also has this much more rock chic look.'

RALPH SMITH, CORNUCOPIA VINTAGE, LONDON

Right: Shopping in Knightsbridge, London, September 2006.

London, September 2006.

Bella Freud Charity
evening, 2006.

'SHE CAME TO AN EVENT I DID AND SHE WAS WEARING A PAIR OF WHITE JEANS. WE'D ONLY SEEN LIZ HURLEY IN THEM (AT THAT TIME). BUT KATE SOMEHOW LOOKED VERY PUNK IN THEM, OR VERY QUERELLE DE BREST [A FASSBINDER MOVIE BASED ON JEAN GENET'S 1947 HOMOEROTIC NOVEL ABOUT SAILORS] AND THEN EVERYONE WAS SUDDENLY INTO WHITE JEANS. I REMEMBER LOOKING AT HER THAT NIGHT AND THINKING "WHITE JEANS! HOW DOES SHE DO IT?". IT WAS JUST SO RADICAL.'
Bella Freud, designer, London

'She's totally wearing it back to front, it's definitely the one. And also, I think she has some little top on under the whole thing; maybe like a little vest or a little tee under it. Because the draping she's got at the front should be a really low back, and then the front wasn't really high but it was almost straight, a couple inches below the neck... Almost like a boat neck.

It's jersey. Vicky Tiel's pieces weren't complicated or tricky, they weren't super difficult – they were easy to wear party dresses, and the fabrics were simple as well, they weren't very often "spectacular" in that way, there was a lot of jersey not always, but often.

I've had some other coloured ones but most of them are black, and most of them are cocktail dresses, though we've had a couple of long pieces in.

I don't know if it's a really London thing to do – to wear it like that, to kind of dress it down, but I wasn't surprised when I saw Kate wearing it like that... I mean, when she's in here trying things on, she'll be like "yes, I like this, yes, I want to try this one". She's very spontaneous, and I guess she just was like "I'm going to wear it like this" and then did it. And it looks great!'

JARRED CARINS,
DECADES VINTAGE, LA

'The Margaux wedge was designed in 1973. I think this is what Kate loves about them. She knows it's an original design of mine from an era that she loves. They were wearing them at Studio 54 back then. I brought it back again for spring/summer 2005 and had the opportunity to "fine tune" it and make it even more comfortable for partying in, which was a fantastic thing to be able to do. Looks like I got it right because Kate always seems to wear them in the spirit that they were designed for.. when she's out for a good time. You can't get a better nod of approval than that. It's now into it's eighth season and is still the best seller in the collection and that's down to Kate's endorsement of it as a design. She doesn't care that it's a couple of seasons old. She just likes to wear those shoes. God bless her for it.'

TERRY DE HAVILLAND, SHOE DESIGNER, LONDON

Sir Paul McCartney's 65th birthday party, June 2007.

'THIS IS A WHITE HALSTON SPLIT LEG GOWN. HALSTON IS ONE OF KATE'S FAVOURITE DESIGNERS. AMERICAN DESIGNERS ARE GREAT BECAUSE IT'S ABOUT THE WOMAN WHO IS WEARING THE CLOTHES; THE CLOTHES DON'T WEAR YOU. SHE DISCOVERED IT ON THE SHOOT [FOR POP MAGAZINE]. IT WAS BOUGHT BY [STYLIST] ANDREW RICHARDSON. HE CAME IN AND WAS LOOKING FOR SOMETHING FOR KATE AND I SUGGESTED THAT. SHE ALWAYS SAYS SHE DOESN'T WANT TO LOOK LIKE EVERYONE ELSE. KATE KNOWS HOW TO LOOK REALLY SEXY; SHE LOVES ANYTHING THAT'S BARE AND SEDUCTIVE. AND SHE MUST HAVE LOVED THIS, BECAUSE SHE WORE IT FOR HER BIRTHDAY AS WELL... AND THEN FOR PAUL MCCARTNEY'S 64TH BIRTHDAY.'
Keni Valenti, Keni Valenti vintage, New York

# 'KATE MOSS IS THE 21ST CENTURY MARILYN MONROE.' Philip Treacy, milliner, London

going to do proper cedar-lined closets to moth-proof them, but then it would have been just like a corridor, because it's up in an attic. So my friend [interior designer Katy Grove] did it, and now it's like a shop. It's got sofas, a swing chair and a screen you can get dressed behind. It's like a hangout now.' Yet Kate's vast wardrobe told another story.

And sure enough, the pair filmed themselves hanging out in the attic, Pete strumming and singing on his guitar, Kate walking around in a long, ruffled see-through dress, and sitting in the swing chair and interjecting lines of the song 'KP Nuts'. The film was posted publicly on YouTube.

On 11 April 2007 Kate was waiting in the wings for the first of Pete's solo gigs, An Evening with Pete Doherty at East London's Hackney Empire. Pete introduced the song 'What Katie Did', saying, 'I am dedicating this song ...' before the crowd drowned out his voice with chants of 'Kate! Kate! Kate!' Pete responded, 'Yes – to my fiancée.' Kate joined him on stage to sing a chorus of 'La Belle et la Bete'.

Later that night, Kate was pictured hanging upside down out of an upstairs window nonchalantly smoking, while Pete Doherty sat on the windowsill, strumming on a guitar beside her.

So Kate was with the band, and in May Pete flew to Ibiza to model alongside his fiancée for Roberto Cavalli's autumn/winter advertising campaign. 'They are both iconic,' declared Cavalli. 'Free spirits with a strong personality. Stylish, contemporary and a very intense couple.'

With Pete Doherty at the Moet & Chandon Fashion Tribute, London, 2006.

'Kate's a big Ossie Clark fan, particularly of the tailored pieces; the little jacket or big high-waisted trousers. She looks fabulous in them; she puts them on, and even though they're from that 1970s period, it doesn't look like a vintage piece, it looks like it was made for her yesterday. This outfit is classic Kate; in one way it's such a style statement; but Kate makes it look understated, it doesn't look like a big seventies collar.'
MARK BUTTERFIELD, C20 VINTAGE, DEVON, ENGLAND

Pete, he claimed, 'oozes a new, unexpected brand of sensuality'.

Despite his relentless courting of the press, Pete seemed to be gradually falling out of love with the paparazzi. 'If I'm with Kate, getting from the front door to the car is hard enough in itself,' he said in a TV interview. 'You've got twenty people taking a picture of someone coming out of a gate and getting into a car.'

Time alone for the couple was virtually impossible: 'Now and again when it does happen it's all the more special and you cherish it,' he said, giving a glimpse into an all-too-rare stolen moment. 'The other week we went into St James's park at two in the morning, because there was no one [paparazzi] outside [Kate's house], so we hot-footed it into town, saw the black swan, walked by the Palace. And by the time we strolled up Piccadilly, someone had spotted us, and someone had phoned someone and … flocks of paparazzi. It's just the way it is; that's the reality of it.'

The couple made one final, glamorous appearance at Glastonbury 2007. Kate was dressed as a glossy goth in PVC jeans, a black lace Victorian mourning cape, studded belt and knee-high boots and Pete in a grey 1960s-style suit and trilby.

Kate and Pete eventually split later that summer. 'She's had enough of the dirty fingers and whatnot …' said Pete.

But Kate had finally left her own legacy to rock 'n' roll; when Babyshambles' second album, *Shotter's Nation* was released in November 2007, Kate was credited as co-writer on four songs.

The Dorchester,
London,
February 2007.

# 9
## Shop Girl

'I've never done this before.
But I've seen it done for
years and years and years.'
KATE MOSS

'Kate Moss for
Topshop'
launch, London,
May 2007.

'Kate Moss for
Topshop'
launch, London,
May 2007.

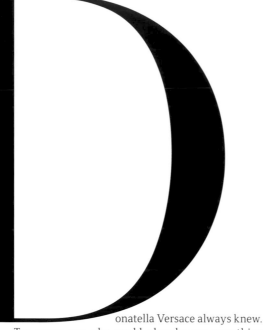

onatella Versace always knew. Ten years ago, she could already see something special in Kate that went beyond a model's usual attitude towards clothes. 'Kate would be fantastic as head of a fashion house, or working behind the image of a company,' she predicted, back in 1999.

But it would be another eight years before Kate would come around to the idea.

Kate approached Topshop boss Philip Green after an evening at the China Tang restaurant at Park Lane's Dorchester hotel, making her business proposal to the fifth richest man in Britain in her usual disarming manner: 'I'm a girl from Croydon, you're a boy from Croydon; why don't we do something together?'

Green assumed it was a joke, but handed Kate his business card just in case, and asked her to come in for a meeting. Within the week, Kate was sitting alone with Sir Philip at his office in Topshop's headquarters. But it would take almost three months for the retail mogul to be convinced that Kate would be fully committed to the venture. 'My starting point was this: does Kate have the desire, drive and potential to build a long-term brand?' he said. 'I wanted her to know that we were not talking about a three-hour photoshoot to publicise a handbag; that this was something completely different.'

The pair finally went public in the front row of Topshop's debut show at London Fashion Week. (Kate had been at her country house in Gloucestershire and Sir Philip had sent a helicopter for her.) Sitting whispering and joking in front of the world's press, Kate's appearance fuelled speculation that she was to be the new face of Topshop's advertising campaign.

Three days later, the launch of the Kate Moss Topshop collection was announced, with Philip Green declaring that the collection would tap into Kate's 'unique position as a true fashion icon'.

The announcement sent shockwaves of excitement around the fashion world. The prospect of a collection of clothing inspired by the most emulated (and private) style icon of the age sparked a burst of anticipation that quickly reached fever pitch.

'I love clothes and I thought it would be fun to do, really,' said Kate. 'I've been modelling for fifteen years; I just thought it was a natural progression.' But privately, the decision was more calculated. At thirty-two, Kate was aware that she couldn't continue modelling forever.

More than that, it was becoming increasingly apparent that Kate's powerful influence on consumers was a valuable and untapped commodity. 'If you wore jeans made by someone you didn't know, and then that person made a lot of money, you'd be thinking, "hang on",' says Grazia's fashion news and features editor Melanie Rickey. 'It's about finding a way to get a slice of the pie. And she's been advised to do that.'

As Kate observed, 'I think they [Topshop] kind

Preview of 'Kate Moss for Topshop' Christmas 2007 collection, October 2007.

of copy me sometimes so I said, "I could give you my stamp and you could get it direct."' The Topshop deal was rumoured to be worth upwards of £3 million, including royalties linked to sales that could push Kate's share to over £10 million.

But Kate was not a fashion designer, and had no desire to be. 'I didn't want to be a designer and have to do shows and all of it,' she said. 'I've seen that stress.'

Instead, Kate would take inspiration from her own wardrobe, referencing her unique personal style and the vintage pieces she had collected over the years. And for the world's most dedicated shopaholic, there was also the ultimate motivation behind creating her own collection: 'I can say, "I want this boot, with that heel",' she says. 'There are things I want that I can't find. Like anyone.'

Kate would also rely on her uncanny knack for predicting the next big thing. 'I see things other people don't sometimes,' she says. 'It's very random but I have this ... radar. I'll think, "Mmm, I fancy wearing a legging," and then, all of a sudden, on the runways it's all leggings. And it's not like we've talked. You just know, it's like a collective consciousness. It's weird. You can't explain it at all.'

And so, ever confident in her taste, Kate was able to employ simple criteria for each garment. 'I wanted to feel that I'd wear it, that I liked it and wanted it.'

Charlie Brear, stylist for Kate's Rimmel advertising,

US launch of 'Kate Moss for Topshop' range at Barney's, New York, May 2007.

'Poiret: King
of Fashion'
Costume Institute
Gala, New York,
May 2007.

says that companies have been tapping into Kate's style expertise for years. 'Kate's opinion and sign-off is crucial; she is always interested and involved and totally part of the team, which is so unlike the usual client–model relationship. I think people really value [her creative input]; it's worth its weight in gold.'

'I'm sure people think she's just a name,' says Mark Butterfield about Kate's role on her Topshop collection. 'She really isn't. She's very much involved with it, and she really wants to make sure everything looks right. And she comes here and chooses the pieces,' he says, referring to C20 Vintage, his vast warehouse of vintage clothing in Devon. (Kate arrives by helicopter, casually jumping out in a trilby, waistcoat and skinny jeans.)

But Kate did have a secret weapon for the range: her close friend Katy England, a respected stylist and long-time creative collaborator of Alexander McQueen.

'[When Kate comes in] Katy England comes too,' says Butterfield. 'She is brilliant because Katy is incredibly professional. Kate will have a great lot of enthusiasm, but Katy, because of her experience with manufacturing, is coming at it from the other side. So Katy will know if something's commercial. She'll say to Kate, "This is what you should wear, but this is great for other people, and it will translate and people will want it." She's got that edge. And when you put that combination together it's a different vibe. It's that ability to cut through [and say] "this is what we need".'

The girls have similar taste, sharing a love of rebellious British designers from McQueen to Westwood. 'Katy's really into [Vivienne] Westwood; she loves that rock 'n' rolly hint in a different way to Kate,' says Butterfield. 'There's a sharper edge to Katy's dressing and style than Kate's. Kate will wear something similar, but softer.'

As with her own wardrobe, Kate understood that a great piece of clothing can be taken to another level with good styling. 'You can take a Victorian jacket and put it with a pair of jeans and spike heels,' she says. 'That's why I work with Katy England. She's a rock chick.'

And so Kate's clothes would have her distinctive twist: giving the clothes an attitude beyond the obvious. 'Just because you're wearing a pretty dress it doesn't have to be pretty-pretty,' says Kate. 'It wasn't how I wanted the clothes to be; that pretty, light kind of thing. I wanted it to be more edgy.'

'Kate's smart,' says Philip Green. 'The six designers, buyers and merchandisers I assigned to work with her found her ideas totally inspiring. She would come into the office every two or three weeks, and I would see her to discuss bigger-picture issues about once a month.'

Kate became such a frequent visitor that she was eventually assigned her own room at the Topshop headquarters. 'My own office! I love it!' she said. 'I want somewhere I can put my mood-boards up!' The room served as little more than a walk-in wardrobe with her collection-in-progress on one side and her various vintage finds – classic tuxedo jackets, stretchy 1980s dresses and 1930s silk gowns – on the other.

Kate was clearly enjoying the research, which had now spread worldwide, as her modelling work and holidays took her from London to LA and Morocco: 'I love going through and finding treasures.' Topshop design consultant Jacqui Markham recalls, 'Two months in we had rails and rails of clothes – ultimately we ended up using only sixty per cent – and still she kept on bringing in new items that had caught her eye.'

Kate was involved in every aspect of the collection, from the advertising campaign images ('I was reading a book of photographs about that club Studio 54 …') to choosing the model for the campaign, Irina Lazareanu, Babyshambles' former drummer, who had recently taken up modelling on Kate's encouragement.

But Kate insisted on being her own fit model for the range. 'Because I've worn so many clothes I know how they should feel when they go on. I could get a fit model but I was like, "No, I'll do it, I'll do it!" I've never done this before so it's kind of a whole new thing. But I've seen it being done for years and years and years, so I know what kind of changes need to be made.'

'K-day', the date that the Kate Moss at Topshop collection was finally launched, on 1 May 2007, brought London's bustling Oxford Circus to a standstill. At the retail chain's flagship store, the biggest fashion shop in Europe, the world's press stood five deep and crowds of onlookers lined the pavements outside. Headlines in the evening papers screamed, 'Moss mania!'

A queue of customers had been waiting for eight hours, and stretched right around the block. The atmosphere was electric with anticipation.

Inside, Kate waited nervously, holding Philip Green's hand, before taking her place in the store's giant windows, hidden behind velvet curtains.

At 8pm, the curtains parted and Kate struck

'We go shopping together, but she doesn't give me advice. We're just normal girls. She just makes it look effortless. Girls all over the world want to follow her and wear what she wears.' KELLY OSBOURNE, FRIEND, LONDON

Sadie Frost at the launch of 'Kate Moss for Topshop' at Barney's, New York, May 2007.

Selma Blair wearing a Kate Moss one shoulder dress, New York, May 2007.

Peaches Geldof wearing 'Kate Moss for Topshop', London, July 2007.

Kelly Osbourne in yellow/purple pansy print Moss dress

Cameron Diaz wearing 'Kate Moss for Topshop', Madrid, June 2007

I did the swallows on Kate Moss's back, and Katy England's "Bobby" tattoo - a wedding present for her partner, Bobby Gillespie. Swallow tattoos are just a really classic design, an old sailor tattoo really. It's quite symbolic, because I think swallows can fly for miles and miles; they're kind of nomadic.  Obviously, Kate's kind of limited in the number of tattoos she can get because of what she does – so it must have been something she really wanted to have...must have been an image she really loves.  And definitely, when she came in, she knew what she wanted – or at least she had an idea, but then I drew the swallows for her, and we talked about where she wanted them to be. And she decided to get them at the bottom of her back.  And then later I saw that they were a part of the Topshop collection, which was amazing. To see it there, taken through all the pieces, almost like a hallmark. It looked great on the sunglasses, because they're so classic as well, such a timeless shape, and so is the swallow, so it was a perfect match. [It was] also on the tags on the jeans, which you can wear on a necklace. And I think on the scarf as well. It's really flattering – to feel like you have inspired someone like that. It was summer 2006, she was wearing the hot-pants and the black boots and black vest she wore through the summer that year at the festivals. Yeah, she's definitely got one or two already, definitely a star somewhere, which she had done a while ago. And then also I think she's got one by Lucien Freud. I don't think it's so much a drawing as just some little markings that he did for her.
SAIRA HUNJAN, THE FAMILY BUSINESS TATTOO SHOP, LONDON

a pose in the store's window in an elegant floor-length red ruffled dress, by Kate Moss for Topshop. The waiting crowds erupted, clapping and cheering and straining to catch a glimpse of her. Kate was illuminated in a snowstorm of camera flashes.

For the majority of the shoppers present, it would have been their first sighting of Kate. 'You're so used to seeing a still of her,' says Charlie Brear. 'In the flesh, she's just as beautiful, but in a kind of different way than you'd expect; she's a bit quirkier, and she's smaller as a person than you'd imagine.'

Kate's pose in the window, before the world's press, lasted for thirteen seconds.

The first customers were let in and inside the store there was pandemonium. Each customer was assigned just twenty minutes to shop in a timeslot denoted by a coloured armband. Each customer was allowed to buy no more than five pieces.

'All the kids want to look like Kate Moss so when she told me about the collaboration I just thought it was logical, really,' said Meg Mathews, one of Kate's group of friends who had turned out to support her on the launch night.

But it wasn't just kids. The customers for Kate's clothes covered a wide range.

'Who else at that grand old age as a model could be doing a Topshop range for teenagers?' says Brear. 'Kate's look is appealing across the board, so there are people in their thirties still buying into that, stood next to a fourteen-year-old in the queue buying the same top. Kate's all for allowing people to dress how they want to dress, in not feeling like they're too old for this.'

Brear says Kate's indefinable age plays a part in her broad appeal. 'When you meet her, she seems so young, like a little girl. She's got quite a giggly laugh, and her voice is quite soft and high. She seems really sweet and young, and we're exactly same age. But that "stuck in lost childhood" thing; that's part of her charm.'

The collection contained all of Kate's greatest hits: from the skinny jeans and waistcoats to shrunken jackets and floral print sundresses, pleated 1950s cocktail dresses and 1930s-style bias-cut silk skirts. She had even included personal touches; the rarely seen swallow tattoo on her back was copied for a logo on the jeans and 1950s-style sunglasses.

The clothes seemed like snapshots from Kate's life so far. The floor-length dress she had worn in the window looked a lot like the see-through vintage dress she wore in the YouTube video with Pete. The little black dress with the strappy

neckline could have been worn next to Johnny on the red carpet at Cannes. The mannish pinstripe trousers might have been bought with Melanie and Corinne at Portobello. The range was not just the essence of Kate's style, but a retrospective.

Some pieces were more literal translations than others. One of the most popular pieces was a copy of a simple cotton sundress, printed with multi-coloured pansies by 1960s label Bus Stop by Lee Bender, that Kate had been spotted wearing in New York in 2005. Vintage dealer Emma Peel observed, 'They've copied the dress exactly, even down to getting the print copied and the detailing around the neck and on the sleeves.' However, she noted the style 'is now a bum-skimming mini dress'. Clearly, not everyone was going to be a fan of Kate's resurrected vintage styles.

When the collection launched in Barney's in New York a week later, Julie Gilhart, the store's fashion director, paid the range the ultimate compliment: 'It feels like you walked into Kate's closet and picked all the best pieces.'

Soon Kate's clothes started appearing on Hollywood's best-dressed celebrities, from Cameron Diaz to Nicole Richie and Selma Blair. Kate had become the style icon of style icons.

Contributing to the line's popularity, Kate wore the range herself, not just for the launch night but pretty much ever day afterwards, incorporated with the designer and vintage clothes from her own wardrobe. Historically, celebrities and designers had never worn pieces from their own high-street collaborations beyond the launch night. Kate's own daily endorsement went beyond merely adding coolness by association; it proved the range's integrity.

Kate chose the black version of her launch night dress to wear to the New York Metropolitan Museum of Art's annual gala, the fashion industry's glitziest party of the year. Alongside celebrities wearing straight-off-the-catwalk outfits and couture creations, Kate held her own in her £195 frock, her hair elegantly piled on top of her head to reveal diamond drop earrings.

Further distilling the essence of her style, Kate had also collaborated on a perfume, which launched soon after the Topshop collection. The perfume, a 'mix of the elegant and risqué', was a blend of glamorous florals like rose, peony and lily of the valley with unexpected touches of patchouli and sandalwood, and spicy pink peppercorn.

Kate attempted to sum up her inimitable and contradictory nature, the inspiration for the perfume: 'I have differences. I'm not always

Kate's fragrance launch, Marrakech, 2007.

'She and her best mate James Brown had been on the website looking at the dresses and rang me at 11.30 at night about a 1970s Grecian-style dress that James had his eye on. Kate had her perfume launch in Morocco the next night, so I shipped it over. She decided she wanted to lop it off to knee length. I got a phone call to check if that was ok (who does that? Certainly not most people in our business!) The dress was absolutely tiny weenie and James helped her into it; by all accounts she had to sit up pretty straight in the car and not breathe too much! But she looked stunning.'
CHARLIE BREAR, THE VINTAGE WEDDING DRESS COMPANY, LONDON

feeling "up" and I'm not always feeling sexy,' she said. 'That's why I wanted to have those mixes. That kind of romanticism is there, with an edgy spike to it.'

In September, Kate's winter collection for Topshop launched, featuring a shrunken cropped biker jacket inspired by Her own vintage one, which was actually a child's jacket, alongside a sweater copied from a Biba black knitted dress given to Kate by hairstylist Sam McKnight, and a metallic skinny-rib cardigan that looked a lot like the one wrapped around Kate's hips at Glastonbury 2005. There was also a very Ossie Clark wide-legged tweed trouser suit and Kate's signature stripy punky jumpers.

A month later, Kate launched a collection of eveningwear. 'Philip says he wants more caaau-uktail dresses,' says Kate, mimicking Sir Philip's accent. The collection referenced Kate's love for embellished vintage evening clothes from the 1920s beaded flapper dresses to 1950s black cocktail dresses and Victorian lace capes. And still the research continued: 'She'd bike over a beaded camisole for us to have a look at,' said Markham.

For the launch night party at Annabel's, surrounded by evening dresses, Kate wore a slinky halterneck all-in-one pantsuit, and a sequinned mini-cape; inspired by 'a beaded cape [I bought] for my best friend for Christmas, and then cheekily borrowed back'. Grace Jones performed

'Swarovski Fashion Rocks', Royal Albert Hall, London, October 2007.

'The dress was based on one Kate has in her collection at home, which is an original 1920s flapper dress. She had it when she was with Johnny Depp, and she wanted it to be the inspiration for this piece for Fashion Rocks. The dress was actually made of quite heavy fabric, because of the weight of the beads. If it had been anything less, anything more light or silky, it would have ripped, because there were so many beads. In total, there were 60,000 Swarovski crystals on the dress. They were in different colours, from clear to grey and golden, and some of them were in a soft green colour as well. There were some tassles that just went straight down and moved with the dress, and then some of them were extra long, and were looped back up again. It took a team of three people two weeks solid work to complete. There was one person working on it full-time and another two part-time, but in terms of man hours, yes it was probably two people's work for two solid weeks. Kate has come in before. She's had things embroidered with people's initials for Christmas presents and things.'
SANA UDDIN, HAND & LOCK, LONDON

a live set, and guests Naomi Campbell, Lily Allen and Chrissie Hynde partied all night.

Kate took her designs to a new level at the annual Prince's Trust Fashion Rocks concert, appearing on the red carpet in a one-off version of the embellished flapper dress from her collection. Hand-beaded in over 60,000 Swarovski crystals, the dress took royal embroiderers Hand & Lock two weeks to sew. 'It was like a dream to use such an amazing amount of Swarovski crystal,' said Kate. 'I get to wear my own amazing couture dress, even if it's just for the night.' After the event, the dress was auctioned for charity.

Kate's fifth collection, A Bohemian Summer, 'Ibiza to Miami, India and Beyond', marked a year of the label, in May 2008. Once again, Kate took inspiration from far and wide; the embroidered red shorts and mirrored waistcoat were copied from a mirrored mini dress of Lila Grace's, the hippy-style fringed waistcoat was 'something wild for the festivals – I'm planning on wearing this tasselled piece with shorts', and a patchwork dress was 'inspired by my collection of unique scarves from around the world. It has a very eclectic feel – I love it!'

Kate was in her element. The first year of the label had been a phenomenal smash hit, with sales hitting £3.5 million in the first week, and the range boosted Topshop's already considerable turnover by 10 per cent in the first six months. The collection was now on sale in twenty-one countries.

'It always surprises me when there is such a reaction to things I do,' Kate says, 'I don't expect people to be like that but I suppose it's always nice.'

'I'm just really pleased she did this,' says Kate's friend and designer Sadie Frost. 'Kate always lacked the confidence to do something outside of modelling, but she needed to find something that would give her fulfilment, and as she's got older she's become more self-confident and more of a shrewd businesswoman.'

For Kate, her label was just beginning, claiming future collections will be 'not just taking stuff from my closet as it is now, but [imagining] what my dream closet would be'.

'It's just so great that she's involved in the whole design process,' says stylist Brana Wolf. 'I recently bumped into Kate in LA, and she was so excited. She's learning the process [of fashion production]; it's a whole new learning experience. [Anyone] can go out and buy clothes, but when you have to produce a collection …'

'She goes around and is looking, which I think is great for her because she does absorb all this style, and she's getting more and more excited about finding ideas.'

'And now there's a purpose to it; she can use all that experience for her own project. She's not just dressing for herself anymore.'

# 10
# Fashionably
# Ever After

'I think it's because I don't follow a trend.
I just have a thrown-together look.'
KATE MOSS

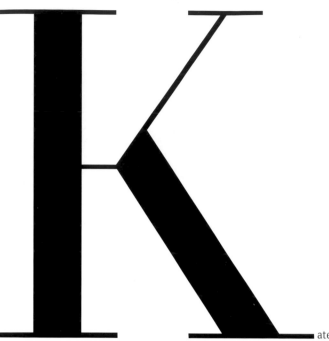

Kate arrived at the opening night party for the Golden Age of Couture exhibition at London's Victoria and Albert Museum, poised and elegant in a floor-sweeping cream satin bias-cut vintage gown with leg o'mutton sleeves, which she and James Brown had found on a vintage website. The look was pure unadulterated glamour: the scarlet lips, the gleaming gown, the tousled gold hair. Kate looked like dishevelled royalty.

But Kate's refined sophistication was short-lived. The dress's tiny waterfall train became entangled in her fellow partygoers' feet, the delicate antique fabric was torn at the shoulder and, worse, there was a huge rip across her bottom. The dress was in tatters.

Unfazed, Kate lifted the dress, tying it in a bow at her hip, and all signs of damage miraculously vanished. But more than that: the dress had been transformed, improved. It now resembled a leggy 1980s cocktail dress. Kate had given the dress a new spin, and everyone present a masterclass in styling. Unstoppable, unshakeable in her own fashion confidence, Kate went on to the Dorchester, partying all night long in the remodelled dress.

'She has no fear!' says stylist Charlie Brear. 'This is a prime example of how Kate views clothes and fashion. With the press all over you … she still has fun with it and refuses to be told what she can and can't do. And always looks amazing.'

Post Topshop, Kate was at a crossroads with her personal style. After years of building up a fiercely individual collection of clothes, her inimitable personal wardrobe was now on sale across the world.

'I think the Topshop thing is disturbing,' says designer Liza Bruce, who argues that perhaps the collection was a little too close to Kate's own style DNA. 'Those clothes – it was her. Your own sense of your self changes a bit. In the [Topshop] window she was a model, but was also herself; the mystery was also lessened a bit. People could get their hands on a part of her.'

Kate also admitted, 'It's so weird selling my own clothes. Who'd have believed it?' The girl who never wanted to look like anyone else had ensured that thousands of women would be walking around in exact copies of her favourite clothes.

In the autumn, just after Kate's third Topshop collection was launched, Bella Freud reissued a limited edition of her 'Ginsberg is God' jumper, which sold out in days. Even Jefferson was spotted wearing one.

Kate's fame was also starting to curtail her shopping habits. As *Vogue* reported, 'Kate does most of her shopping by ordering pieces she likes on shoots, and zipping into little vintage stores.' According to Julien Macdonald, however, 'Steven [Phillips, of Rellick] is the person who picks a lot of Kate's dresses. He sends a bag of clothes over

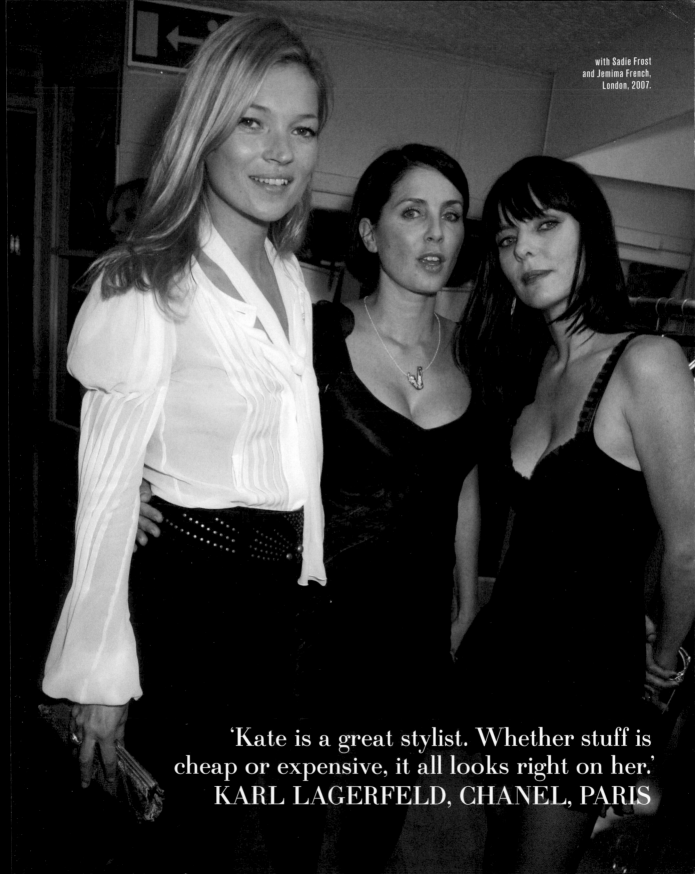

with Sadie Frost
and Jemima French,
London, 2007.

'Kate is a great stylist. Whether stuff is
cheap or expensive, it all looks right on her.'
KARL LAGERFELD, CHANEL, PARIS

to Kate every week. He knows what she likes and what she doesn't like.'

The vintage scene was changing too, and Kate was partly responsible for that. 'Kate always really talked up the places she bought from,' says Tracey Tolkien. 'Very few people do that.' In fact two of her favourite hunting grounds, Cornucopia and Steinberg and Tolkien are now closed. (The latter is set to reopen in Los Angeles.)

And while, in the early years, Kate was able to rifle around Portobello and find pieces by distinguished designers like Ossie Clarke and Biba for pocket-money prices, market stalls and charity shops today have become increasingly full of recent cast-offs from the high-street and budget retailers.

Real vintage is now recognised as collectible, and valuable. Jumbled boutiques have been replaced by sleek upmarket vintage stores like Rellick in West London and Decades in Los Angeles. 'One pays a premium to shop at a store like Decades,' admits Cameron Silver, Decades owner. 'It is a luxury to do that. But you can't necessarily acquire those things at Portobello Market.'

Kate was starting to sound a little nostalgic for the old days. 'I'd visit jumble sales in Croydon and get bags full of clothes – like bin-liners for a fiver. I can't do that now.'

'Kate started as a model and has turned into a global icon,' says Domenico Dolce. 'Suddenly,

London,
autumn
2007.

London,
September
2007.

she became a legend. It seemed that we couldn't do without Kate … How does she wear clothes? Which are her favourite restaurants and clubs?'

Kate thinks 'its flattering' that women want to follow her look. 'I think it's because I don't follow a trend. I just have a thrown-together look.'

Right now, Kate's 'thrown-together look' revolves around a slick, pulled-together uniform of jackets, boots and 'It' bags. She adopts the (big) bag of the moment in the current season's colour, from the YSL Downtown in dove-grey leather to the Mulberry Bayswater in apple-green alligator and Chanel's Coco Cabas Tote in shiny black patent. She wears cropped vintage furs, sharply tailored tuxedo jackets or fitted blazers with kicked-in boots: tall boots with high heels, suede-fringed ankle boots, short flat leather boots or stretch suede over-the-knee boots.

'She's very discreet with what she wears, although she's a fashion trendsetter,' says Fran Cutler. 'She's got integrity and style. She won't wear something outrageous just to get photographed.'

Kate's choices are so directional and influential that when she wears a new pair of jeans it becomes a major news story for the fashion press. 'When Kate first wore the [flared] J-Brand jean, it was my mission for the day to find out where it was from,' says *Grazia*'s fashion news and features editor, Melanie Rickey. 'And subsequently that style was copied by every high-

Kate's 34th
birhthday, 2008.

'KATE IS NEVER A FASHION VICTIM. FOR ME SHE IS THE ULTIMATE MODERN GIRL AND THE MOST STYLISH OF THEM ALL.'
Karl Lagerfeld, Chanel, Paris

street store and became a major trend.'

'There's a certain group of people in London who show us the next level of what's going to be interesting to wear,' says J-Brand's Susie Crippen. 'Kate's definitely one of those people.'

The Moss effect is now easily quantifiable. According to Lucy Pinter and Flora Evans, the designers behind Superfine, 'Kate Moss has, without doubt, had a huge influence on our success. She was always the girl that we wanted to wear our clothes. We started Superfine because we were bored of LA jeans; we wanted skinny, sexy, rock 'n' roll London jeans. Kate seemed to sum that up for us.'

'Kate now wears a lot of Superfine jeans,' says Rickey, 'and they happen to be social friends of hers; Flora's husband is Ringo Starr's son. So she gives support to her friends too, in subtle ways.'

When her long-time friend James Brown launched his haircare range at the end of 2007 (backed by Davinia Taylor), Kate was on hand to make it a success, appearing in the advertising campaign.

'Kate has a lot of help from James Brown,' says Julien Macdonald. 'He is The Wardrobe Mistress. He regularly goes shopping for Kate and tells her what to wear. James Brown is Kate Moss. He dressed Kate.'

'I remember bumping into James once at Kings Cross station at seven in the morning. He was wearing a three-piece tweed suit with a cashmere polo neck,' says Lee Williams, an actor and long-time friend of James. 'I have a feeling he was quite influential in Kate's style.' But James is modest about his contribution to Kate's success: 'That's the impression, that I am the gay best friend who lets her shine, [but] it's her keeping my feet on the ground!'

With perfect timing, Kate changed her hair soon after the James Brown London haircare range launched. The chunky fringe cut by James was, he claimed, partly inspired by Michelle Pfeiffer's bob in *Scarface*. 'We got together and just decided to do it,' he said. 'Kate hasn't had a fringe for years, but it makes her look fresh and sexy, and I just love the shoulder-length cut as well.'

The new haircut made its debut in the prestigious YSL advertising campaign, in which Kate showed off a new sharper, edgier image.

Whether it was deliberate or accidental, the haircut was reminiscent not only of Pfeiffer, but also of Anita Pallenberg in her 1960s heyday. In fact, the winter saw Kate embrace Anita's style wholeheartedly, in a uniform of skinny jeans,

over-the-knee boots and oversized furs. 'Anita really gets the idea of the glamour and rock and roll of a big fur jacket and skinny jeans,' says stylist Kira Joliffe. 'It's so old school, she's been doing that for forty years; there's a legacy going on there.' Endlessly emulated, Kate still had sartorial heroes of her own.

By December, Kate's take on Anita's style hit a high, when she attended the Led Zeppelin reunion concert, wearing a black and white striped oversized Fendi fur. Under the coat, she wore a black leotard with sheer tights and tall leather boots. Later, she partied with the Presleys, Naomi, Liam Gallagher, Mick Jagger and Led Zeppelin. The outfit, and the attitude, were Pallenberg personified.

'Anita is an old rock chick; she's been here and done that,' says vintage dealer Jeff Ihenacho. 'Kate looks to her for inspiration. When Kate is in her grungy look, in her rock chick look, it's Anita in her heyday.'

The Topshop range may have provided a temporary sartorial setback, but Kate's style never stands still. Her research for the range led her to discover yet another vintage designer: Thea Porter. '[Porter's] aesthetic is unconventional and eccentric; Kate adores her clothes,' says vintage dealer Mark Butterfield, who explains that the dresses are tightly fitted to the torso and then wafting and billowy from the waist, 'and there was a little keyhole on the bust, so they're quite sexy too: big flowing romantic skirts with mixed prints – the typical rich hippie look. Thea Porter was really the first person to do that rock 'n' roll vibe. Kate was saying, "You'd have to be some really groovy hippy to wear that," and she was right, because Thea Porter was making individual pieces for rock stars' wives and Kate just loves all that; it's that vibe which she always injects into [her looks].'

As usual Kate was seeing beyond aesthetics, to an attitude. 'I guess one of the things is, she's in this industry where everything is regimented, and Kate's kind of rebelled against that,' says Jarred Carins, of Decades vintage in LA. 'And that's really her vibe, and those [Thea Porter] dresses are like that, too. They're really easy to wear, and the same with Ossie Clarke's tailoring.'

'I think Kate has a healthy disrespect for clothes,' says Butterfield. 'She doesn't see them as precious things. But then, she's got the pick of everything hasn't she? People are always throwing stuff at her, left, right and centre, because it's great for them to have Kate Moss wearing it.

Far left: Shopping in New York, November 2007. Left: London, November 2007.

Far left: Christmas shopping in London's West End, December 2007. Below: London, autumn 2007.

'She came in with Fran Cutler, and actually that was why I recognised her — because Fran is quite a regular as well — and I realised that the person with her was Kate Moss It's a 1920's gold sequined jacket, actually quite a silvery gold, and the light reflects on to it, making the sequins look all sorts of different shades. In fact, those very old sequins used to be made of gelatine, so it's amazing they've survived. It would originally have been a part of a set; quite possibly the coat would have gone with a flapper dress to match. Obviously they've become separated somewhere along the way. I love the way Kate wears them with skinny jeans and a vest — it's a sort of reinvention of an old piece, it gives it a new lease of life. She wears things brilliantly, and looks fabulous in whatever she wears... in vintage clothes or in new things.

She knows exactly what she wants when she comes in. Sort of, you know, steams around the rails, and licks things up, putting them over her arms, and the goes off into the changing room. And that time, when she came out, one or two things were rejected because they didn't fit, but she bought the rest of it. I think on that occasion she must have bought about 30 pieces or so. And then, when she came to the counter, we'd just brought in a little pearl brooch, which we had on the counter, and she came out of the changing room wearing one of the 1920s lawn blouses she'd chosen and her little waistcoat, and her eyes just lighted on this brooch and she said, "Oooh, I shall have to have that, it's just like my [swallow] tattoo" and she pinned it on her waistcoat then and there.'

ANNIE MOSS, ANNIE'S VINTAGE, LONDON

Linda McCartney exhibition, London.

And I'm sure from that point of view she sees so much, [that for her to choose a garment] it has to be something that catches her [eye] in a different way.'

Kate's private life was moving on too. At the beginning of the autumn, Kate was spotted with The Kills' guitarist Jamie Hince. She had been introduced to him by Jefferson, who had previously dated Jamie's bandmate Alison Mosshart. Kate and Jamie were virtually inseparable, going from pub to gig to party to club, night after night.

Meanwhile Pete Doherty had started briefly dating Irina Lazareanu, the model for Kate's first Topshop range (and whom Doherty had known since his teens). Kate and Lila moved out of the North London home she had shared with Doherty at the end of the year, moving in with Davinia Taylor in nearby St Johns Wood.

Although Kate claims, 'I'm crap with interiors. I've got a theory that because I lived out of a suitcase for so long … I find it difficult to make decisions about things I can't pack', her furnishings tell a different story. The authentic pieces reveal her mix-and-match dishevelled sophistication: a mink-grey velvet curved Chesterfield sofa, a bottle-green velvet chaise longue, a regency-style black stool and mirror studded with pearl flowers, brown leather and chrome modernist dining room chairs, a lime-washed Louis XV chair from her pink bedroom, and mugs featuring Warhol's Double Elvis screen print and Sid Vicious's police mug shot.

David Tang says Kate 'has a great sense of style – if she goes into a [hotel] room she doesn't like, she'll change the furniture around or drape fabric over a lamp'.

'[The Topshop range] made her be more interested in everything on a design level,' says Brana Wolf. 'I think you'll see her expanding beyond fashion into home – "the world of Kate".'

Behind closed doors, the world of Kate is a laid-back affair. 'The real Kate likes hanging out at home with her family,' says James Brown, 'cooking the meanest Sunday roast you'll ever taste, then flopping on the sofa and watching telly.' Kate counts her blessings for her family life: 'Jefferson's a great dad; somehow this was Mother Nature's intervention.'

Lila has inherited her mother's passion for clothes. 'She says, "Mum, do you think this is a good look?" Then she has a fashion crisis,' Kate reveals. 'I say, "You'll wear what I tell you!" We lay the clothes out before she goes to bed, but she goes, "Mum, I need options."' Lila was recently spotted trying on a diamante The Who T-shirt.

Kate insists, 'I wouldn't want her to be a model. I don't think it's the best industry really for young girls.' But at four years old, Lila was playing dress-up with Donatella Versace on one of Kate's advertising campaign shoots. Donatella had put a weave in her hair. 'Lila was [flicking her hair] and I was

'She just bought them! We were so teeny tiny at that time, and she must have gotten them from a store in LA. And I remember Jeff, my business partner called me and I literally could not breathe – and he was saying "she's been seen in the jeans!" and I was like "wait! Let me have this moment!" It was such a massive compliment, a real solidifying moment. When she bought the Love Story pair, it just sold out in every single store in LA. You look at what she's wearing and think "I can do that!" When I saw her in the Love Story, I was like, "I don't even have those jeans! I need some! I have like, 700 pairs of them downstairs!" Style is more about what the person is like inside. And if you think about the idea of freedom, and breeziness and this exotic and chic life she has, it shows in how she wears things. She just kind of epitomises that kind of style.'
SUSIE CRIPPEN, J BRAND, LOS ANGELES

'The Golden Age of Couture Gala', V&A Museum, London, September 2007.

Black tie gala dinner, New York, November 2007.

Celebrating Sir David Tang's Knighthood with Kelly Osbourne, Dorchester Hotel, London.

Leaving Soho House, London, April 2008.

'I LOVE THE WAY KATE WEARS MY FEATHERED WAISTCOAT. SHE IS SUCH AN ENIGMA... ALWAYS SURPRISING AND SIMPLY UNIQUE.' Ann Demeulemeester

like "Oh … my … God!"'

Kate still lives in London, spending her nights in her local pub. 'Kate always seems to perpetuate the idea that she's just a normal girl who has an extraordinary life,' says Rickey. In March 2008, Kate appeared behind the wheel of a traditional vintage black London taxi, which she used to ferry her mates to and from the pub. 'Kate is more fun than anyone I know,' says James Brown.

Kate's sense of fun has led to an as yet unseen vast and spectacular archive of clothes. 'She came in and bought an original costume from the Folies Bergère,' says Tracey Tolkien, 'a beaded basque and can-can skirt with a hat trimmed in marabou with a champagne glass on top. A very historical piece; we had come across the collection of pieces. I think she was thinking, "I don't know where I'll wear it." But she was really just enjoying it, letting her imagination run wild. I think you have to want to imagine the person who wore it and the adventures they had in it; you have to have that romantic attitude towards it.'

'What's great about her, [is that] she's quite a light-hearted character who has fun in her life,' says Rickey. Kate's relaxed attitude to cameras, learnt early on from constant observance by Corinne Day and Mario Sorrenti, has endured. 'She seems to be able to disassociate herself from the press attention,' says Rickey. 'I think she's so self-assured in her looks; in Miami on holiday what came through was her just having a laugh with her kids.'

196

On holiday with Jamie Hince, 2007.

Now thirty-four, and a mother, after almost two decades in fashion, Kate's career shows no sign of slowing down. 'For my spring/summer 2008 campaign, I wanted a woman,' says Donna Karan, 'someone who could tell a story. Kate has that depth of experience.'

But Kate refuses to grow up and refuses to alter her dress sense as she gets older, saying, 'Ha! No! I still think I'm seventeen.'

'That sweetness is really one of the reasons she's had such longevity,' says Liza Bruce. 'She's sexy, but she's never really changed into a proper woman. Despite becoming a mother, and having this long career, she doesn't ever seem to be tired, or to want to go home, and that's really important. She's very good with people. She enjoys people.'

'She looks exactly the same,' says vintage dealer Virginia Bates, who has known Kate for over fifteen years. 'I don't think she's ever changed. And not compromising for your age is definitely the mark of a great style icon.'

But perhaps the true test of a style icon is time. Kate's endless sartorial adventures have already inspired countless trends. And her simple love for clothing will ensure that Kate's wardrobe will always be worth watching.

According to Tom Ford, the best may yet lie ahead. 'As I know her mother, who is equally stunning at sixty, I have a feeling that Kate will be embodying the spirit of the times for decades to come.'

# EPILOGUE
# SO WAS KATE BORN COOL? PERHAPS.

But the fashion education of Kate Moss has been a long and collaborative journey.

Just as Elizabeth Taylor was born in London but raised in the old Hollywood studio system to become the last great silver-screen icon, Kate was born in London but raised by the fashion industry to become the great style icon of this age.

James Brown and Steven Phillips at Rellik have dressed her, found clothes for her and contributed to her style ('Kate has a lot of gay best friends,' says Julien Macdonald). Vintage dealers like Tracey Tolkien and Mark Steinberg have scoured the world and the ages for the most beautiful clothes for her.

Corinne Day and Melanie Ward contributed an education in the unadulterated, intrinsic value and joy of clothes – any clothes – for their own sake, and designers like Vivienne Westwood, Alexander McQueen and John Galliano opened her eyes to the rarefied world of fashion and a new way of dressing.

Her boyfriends, from Johnny Depp and Jefferson Hack to Pete Doherty and beyond, showed her that to look cool, you have to be cool. And as she has grown older, she has looked to her own style idol, Anita Pallenberg, to inspire her and show her the way.

And in the midst of it all has been Kate. 'You can't explain it all,' says Liza Bruce. 'It's so dynamic. It's kind of destiny.' So she was always going to get there, but this at last is what Kate has become: a style icon.

'Years and years from now, when you look back on pictures of Kate you'll get an idea of what our time was about,' says Brana Wolf. 'You'll understand where fashion was at the time, because they all want to wear what Kate Moss wears.'

# CONTRIBUTORS

| | |
|---|---|
| Alber Elbaz | Lanvin |
| Ann Demeulemeester | Designer |
| Annie Moss | Annie's Vintage Clothing |
| Bella Freud | Bella Freud |
| Brana Wolf | Stylist |
| Britt Ekland | Actress |
| Cameron Silver | Decades Inc |
| Charlie Brear | The Vintage Wedding Dress Company |
| Dan Macmillan | Zoltar the Magnificent |
| Darimeya | Designer |
| David Ross | Photographer |
| Domenico Dolce | Dolce & Gabbana |
| Donna Karan | Donna Karan |
| Farah Pidgeon | Southpaw |
| Fran Cutler | Friend |
| Inacia Ribeiro | Clements Ribeiro |
| Jarred Cairns | Decades Inc |
| Jeff Ihenacho | One of a Kind |
| John Bland | John Bland |
| Julien Macdonald | Julien Macdonald |
| Karl Lagerfeld | Chanel |
| Katie Grand | POP magazine |
| Katy Rodriguez | Katy Rodriguez, Resurrection Vintage |
| Kelly Osborne | Friend |
| Keni Valenti | Keni Valenti |
| Kira Jolliffe | Cheap Date |
| Lee Williams | Actor |
| Leslie Verrinder | Leslie Verrinder |
| Liza Bruce | Liza Bruce |
| Lori Goldstein | Stylist |
| Louise Mazzilli | Voyage |
| Manolo Blahnik | Manolo Blahnik |
| Marc Jacobs | Marc Jacobs |
| Mario Sorrenti | Photographer |
| Mark Butterfield | C20 Vintage Fashion |
| Matthew Williamson | Matthew Williamson |
| Melanie Rickey | Grazia |
| Melanie Ward | Stylist |
| Michael Boadi | Hairdresser |
| Philip Treacy | Milliner |
| Ralph Smith | Cornucopia |
| Rich Cornucopia | Cornucopia |
| Rita Watnik | Lily et Cie |
| Saira Hunjan | The Family Business Tattoo Shop |
| Sarna Uddin | Hand and Lock |
| Stefano Gabbana | Dolce & Gabbana |
| Stuart Hammond | Stuart Hammond |
| Sue Stemp | Sue Stemp |
| Susie Crippen | J Brand |
| Tahira Conliffe | Black Betty PR |
| Tanya Sarne | Founder, Ghost. |
| Terry de Havilland | Terry de Havilland |
| Tom Ford | Tom Ford International |
| Tracey Tolkien | Seinberg and Tolkien |
| Virginia Bates | Virginia |

The following publications and websites have been particularly inspirational in the writing of this book; *Dazed and Confused, Elle* (UK), *The Face, Grazia* (UK), *Harper's Bazaar* (US), *i-D, Interview*, showstudio.com, *Spin*, The *Times, V magazine*, and *W*. And in particular, the American, British and French editions of *Vogue*.

Thank you to the following for giving permission to use the photos in this book: Alan Davidson, Alpha, Barcroft, Big Pictures, Camera Press, Catwalking.com, Corbis, David Ross, Eagle Press, Express Syndication, Eyevine, Film Magic, Getty Images, Goff Inf, Landmark Media, LFI, Matrix, Pacific Coast News, PA Photos, Patrick McMullan, Retna, Reuters, Rex Features, Solar Pix, Splash News, UK Press, Wenn, Wire Image and Xposure.

# CONTRIBUTORS

| | |
|---|---|
| Alber Elbaz | Lanvin |
| Ann Demeulemeester | Designer |
| Annie Moss | Annie's Vintage Clothing |
| Bella Freud | Bella Freud |
| Brana Wolf | Stylist |
| Britt Ekland | Actress |
| Cameron Silver | Decades Inc |
| Charlie Brear | The Vintage Wedding Dress Company |
| Dan Macmillan | Zoltar the Magnificent |
| Darimeya | Designer |
| David Ross | Photographer |
| Domenico Dolce | Dolce & Gabbana |
| Donna Karan | Donna Karan |
| Farah Pidgeon | Southpaw |
| Fran Cutler | Friend |
| Inacia Ribeiro | Clements Ribeiro |
| Jarred Cairns | Decades Inc |
| Jeff Ihenacho | One of a Kind |
| John Bland | John Bland |
| Julien Macdonald | Julien Macdonald |
| Karl Lagerfeld | Chanel |
| Katie Grand | POP magazine |
| Katy Rodriguez | Katy Rodriguez, Resurrection Vintage |
| Kelly Osborne | Friend |
| Keni Valenti | Keni Valenti |
| Kira Jolliffe | Cheap Date |
| Lee Williams | Actor |
| Leslie Verrinder | Leslie Verrinder |
| Liza Bruce | Liza Bruce |
| Lori Goldstein | Stylist |
| Louise Mazzilli | Voyage |
| Manolo Blahnik | Manolo Blahnik |
| Marc Jacobs | Marc Jacobs |
| Mario Sorrenti | Photographer |
| Mark Butterfield | C20 Vintage Fashion |
| Matthew Williamson | Matthew Williamson |
| Melanie Rickey | Grazia |
| Melanie Ward | Stylist |
| Michael Boadi | Hairdresser |
| Philip Treacy | Milliner |
| Ralph Smith | Cornucopia |
| Rich Cornucopia | Cornucopia |
| Rita Watnik | Lily et Cie |
| Saira Hunjan | The Family Business Tattoo Shop |
| Sarna Uddin | Hand and Lock |
| Stefano Gabbana | Dolce & Gabbana |
| Stuart Hammond | Stuart Hammond |
| Sue Stemp | Sue Stemp |
| Susie Crippen | J Brand |
| Tahira Conliffe | Black Betty PR |
| Tanya Sarne | Founder, Ghost. |
| Terry de Havilland | Terry de Havilland |
| Tom Ford | Tom Ford International |
| Tracey Tolkien | Seinberg and Tolkien |
| Virginia Bates | Virginia |

The following publications and websites have been particularly inspirational in the writing of this book; *Dazed and Confused*, *Elle* (UK), *The Face*, *Grazia* (UK), *Harper's Bazaar* (US), *i-D*, *Interview*, showstudio.com, *Spin*, *The Times*, *V magazine*, and *W*. And in particular, the American, British and French editions of *Vogue*.

Thank you to the following for giving permission to use the photos in this book: Alan Davidson, Alpha, Barcroft, Big Pictures, Camera Press, Catwalking.com, Corbis, David Ross, Eagle Press, Express Syndication, Eyevine, Film Magic, Getty Images, Goff Inf, Landmark Media, LFI, Matrix, Pacific Coast News, PA Photos, Patrick McMullan, Retna, Reuters, Rex Features, Solar Pix, Splash News, UK Press, Wenn, Wire Image and Xposure.